Popper's Legacy

Popper's Legacy
Rethinking Politics, Economics
and Science

Raphael Sassower

McGill-Queen's University Press
Montreal & Kingston • Ithaca

192
P8 3zsa

© Raphael Sassower, 2006

H

ISBN-13: 978-0-7735-3175-8   ISBN-10: 0-7735-3175-0 (hardcover)
ISBN-13: 978-0-7735-3176-5   ISBN-10: 0-7735-3176-9 (paperback)

Legal deposit third quarter 2006
Bibliothèque nationale du Québec

Published simultaneously outside North America
by Acumen Publishing Limited

McGill-Queen's University Press acknowledges the financial support of
the Government of Canada through the Book Publishing Development
Program (BPIDP) for its activities

Library and Archives Canada Cataloguing in Publication

Sassower, Raphael
   Popper's legacy : rethinking politics, economics and science /
Raphael Sassower.

Includes bibliographical references and index.
ISBN-13: 978-0-7735-3175-8   ISBN-10: 0-7735-3175-0 (bound)
ISBN-13: 978-0-7735-3176-5   ISBN-10: 0-7735-3176-9 (pbk.)

   1. Popper, Karl R. (Karl Raimund), Sir, 1902–1994.   I. Title.

B1649.P64S22
2006   192   C2006-902315-8

Typeset by Graphicraft Ltd., Hong Kong.
Printed and bound by Cromwell Press, Trowbridge.

Contents

v

Contents

Acknowledgements

I would like to thank Joseph Agassi, Stanley Aronowitz, Steve Fuller and my editor, Tristan Palmer, for their helpful comments and suggestions. A revised section of Chapter 3 (on Haraway and Popper) appeared as Chapter 4 in my previously published *Cultural Collisions: Postmodern Technoscience* (Routledge, 1995). As always, I would like to thank the officials at my home institution, the University of Colorado at Colorado Springs, for staying out of my intellectual way.

Introduction

Karl Popper has been a central figure in the European intellectual life of the twentieth century, yet relatively ignored for most of his life. Perhaps one reason for this relative neglect of his ideas has been his move from Vienna to escape the Nazis all the way to New Zealand where he spent the war years (World War II). He eventually made it to Britain with a position at the London School of Economics, rather than the more prestigious universities of Oxford or Cambridge. He was known by his contemporaries, but was not the first choice (and at times not chosen at all) to give keynote speeches at conferences. Perhaps his legacy exemplifies the stereotype of the wandering Jew. Unlike Odysseus, who had a home to go back to, the wandering Jews had to move from point to point, finding refuge from one danger only to find another in their new homes. They were victims of their enemies for centuries, whether the Catholic Inquisition in Spain in the fifteenth century or the Russian pogroms in the nineteenth century. The more they tried to assimilate to their newfound homes, the more they realized that their difference would come up at some point to haunt them, and to provide the excuse for the natives to persecute and eventually expel them. Whether the natives were enlightened or not, as was the case in the British Isles in the sixteenth century, the Jews had to go! No matter how hard they tried, the Jews remained outsiders, foreigners, untrustworthy residents.

Instead of exploring in detail the historical and cultural causes for the phenomenon of wandering Jews, I would like to link Popper's own wanderings to theirs (despite the fact that his own genealogy stresses his parents' conversion). Perhaps the one who wanders has

I

the disadvantage of losing one's bearings and roots, one's foundation; but that, too, can have its own advantages. For example, one is less bound by tradition and more willing to explore new ideas and options. Similarly, one is more critical of everything, including one's own background and ideas, because the incessant changes one experiences as one moves from place to place can be enriching and at times contradictory, allowing for revisions and change of opinion from the complacency of one's heritage. And finally, one is forced to be always an insider who is at heart an outsider and thus one is forced to keep wandering. On those occasions when the wandering is less physical, when there is some stability in one's residence, there still is intellectual and psychological wandering, an ongoing shifting from one thought to another, from one ideological framework to another. Perhaps this is no different from Socrates' taunt that the unexamined life is not worth living; perhaps it is Odysseus' journey to foreign lands only to return home a different man.

In the case of Popper, historical circumstances beyond his control forced him to become a wandering (non-)Jew. As he moved from one continent to another, he must have thought of his own fate in psychological terms, but translated it into more cognitive ones. Along the way, he found like-minded fellow-travellers, European intellectuals whose own refugee status must have affected their ideas on how to protect the individual, the wandering Jew, against the authority of the state whose nationalistic tendencies can flare into xenophobia at the drop of a hat. How can we allow the Jews to live in our midst without them threatening our own identity? How can we make sure the Jews follow our laws and customs without losing their own identity? The nineteenth-century liberal tradition in Europe struggled to come up with solutions to these problems, since they were real practical problems, and not mere theoretical puzzles. Popper is a product of this tradition and of these experiences. Perhaps his association with the Austrian School, for example, helped assure a perception of him as a reactionary conservative thinker who would support the political and social status quo rather than provide the philosophical guidelines for new revolutionary ideas and institutions. But at heart he always remained a staunch liberal in the classical sense of the protection of the rights of individuals (with a minimal government for legal protection of the least fortunate).

In some ways, I would like to debunk some of the misconceptions associated with Popper and explain how his legacy over the past century and into the present offers us a fresh look and perhaps a useful foundation (with a qualified sense of a foundation, always provisional and always open to critical evaluation) with which to approach our present political situations and our future actions in correcting the mistakes of our ancestors. It is true that Popper's most lasting legacy is related to his methodological discussions in the philosophy of science, using, as he did, the record of the history of philosophy with a clear appreciation of the metaphysical elements that bring about the thinking and practices of the scientific community. However, my own concern is to link this part of his legacy with another part, namely his view on social piecemeal engineering (as expressed in his political writings) as an alternative to utopian thinking (which he found to be simultaneously intellectually dogmatic and potentially violent). As will become clear from the rest of the book, I see his legacy as a whole, trying not to isolate this or that statement, this or that idea from the rest of his work.

I should also like to emphasize from the beginning that my own fascination with Popper's legacy is twofold. On the one hand, I find the core of his ambitious and innovative works to be ethical in nature (worrying about the proper and optimal behaviour of individuals within institutional structures), and on the other hand, I am interested in how his own ideas are neither positivist nor reductionist, but fully in synch with other philosophical and intellectual movements, such as feminism and postmodernism, which concede some sense of realism to our natural surroundings. Some of his most ardent disciples would object to my loose interpretation and keep him within the fold of critical rationalism in its original formulation or its later variants. Yet, to have a lasting legacy that pervades the whole western intellectual landscape, I think it is more fruitful to stretch his views and ideas and illustrate the extent to which they predate and prefigure later developments (and as such overlap more than contradict them). I prefer this strategy so as to make Popper's legacy more widely appreciated by the intellectual world, and give him credit where credit is due.

Popper has gained some prominence over the past few years, perhaps in large part because of the endorsement of someone like George Soros, the billionaire who attributes his fortune to his ideas, and this, too, provides an opportunity to revisit his legacy. Most American billionaires are content to present a (Cartesian look-alike) self-legitimation posture ("I am rich, therefore I am smart"), rather than contend with great ideas or great books. With hyper-capitalism permeating the entire globe (as one can see in the emergence of the Chinese economy), any intellectual foundation or pretence that legitimizes focusing on the marketplace is worthy of re-examination. Popper's legacy drew the attention of a few disciples during his lifetime, and later on some of their students laboured diligently to make his work more common and even part of the academic curriculum by the end of the twentieth century. But at the dawn of the twenty-first century, Popper deserves an irreverent critique, perhaps owing to, and not despite, his increasing popularity and prestige in the intellectual community and among the educated public. If his ideas merit examination in this century, it is partially in light of the conditions of the previous century, which gave rise to them.

Moreover, if financial tycoons end up underwriting centres and foundations, even whole universities, then we should really worry about what has driven them to this unprecedented hero worship. That saints and religious icons inspire higher learning is quite common; but rarely have philosophers been lionized beyond a library name or a sculpture somewhere on campus, a collection of essays or an international conference. Popper, it appears, has touched a raw nerve: what is it about his thought that is both inspiring and bewildering, worthy of critical analysis that defies the standard categories of good and bad, left and right, liberal and conservative? If sufficient attention is paid to the actual record of his writings, he could be an inspiring thinker for multiple movements, being, as he is, first and foremost a pluralist at heart. He has rejected the standard opposition, for example, between relativism (the view that anything is just as good as anything else) and absolutism or foundationalism (the view that that there are definite and specific core principles according to which everything must be judged) in favour of a middle ground that would allow one to judge according to a set of criteria but be tolerant of differences (called critical rationalism).

There are a few intellectual "schools" to which Popper may belong, and in my view he in fact stands in between them, rather than in the midst of any of them. This might be true of any thinker, if one ascribes originality and uniqueness to his or her thought and then tries to undermine that ascription. But Popper's case is more interesting from a sociological standpoint, as mentioned before, since no one wanted to count him as a member of their group until his fame and reputation became such that everyone wanted to claim him. For example, is Popper part of the Vienna Circle? If yes, in what sense? (The standard answer is that he is a positivist or a metaphysical realist). If not, why? (The standard answer is that he offered a methodological alternative to positivism by rejecting certainty and Truth as ultimate goals for scientific research, and proposed putative truths as worthy of ongoing investigation). Would it not be odd to count him as part of that movement, while acknowledging his disputes with, among others, Hans Reichenbach and Ludwig Wittgenstein? On some level, Popper contributed to the demise of the Vienna Circle, moving it to face epistemological positions that required a different perspective on the status of truth. On another level, Popper is still associated with an epistemological positivist agenda despite his ontological convictions, because of his insistence that every theory or conjecture be put to strict empirical testing (perhaps closer to Moritz Schlick's original formulation of epistemology and scientific methodology).

Likewise, Popper has been associated with the kind of neo-classical (conservative, for some) economics of the Friedrich von Hayek clan, namely, the rekindling of the Austrian School. In lumping him with this group, there has been a great interest in using his ideas to rebuff any claim for socialism, economic and political. This view of economics assumes that there is a trade-off between equality and freedom and that freedom takes precedence, rather than the Marxist (or socialist and later communist in its pure theoretical form) view of equality taking precedence. In order to bolster this ideological agenda, the economists and politicians who favour this version of democracy claim the heritage of Popper's fight against fascism and (Soviet) communism alike by invoking his famous notion of an "open society". The extent to which this appropriation of Popper is accurate is open to debate, as I shall try to explain later. It seems to me that hijacking political ideals in the name of an economic system is overstating the case, and as such is inappropriate. To say that democracy requires freedom is one thing, but to say that it requires a particular market mechanism (such as capitalism) is quite another. Besides, is freedom understood in individualistic terms or in terms of a national constitution or bill of rights?

The third "school" may be understood in terms of some of his disciples, especially those who were his students and research assistants (from William Bartley, Brian Magee and David Miller to Paul Feyerabend, Joseph Agassi and Ian Jarvie), all of whom took Popper's ideas and reworked them to fit more neatly their own concerns with the methodology of the natural and social sciences in general or with their own particular areas of research, such as anthropology. Within this group of scholars one can find a bit of defensiveness on behalf of the "master" so that a critical assessment is always gentle and discreet, chipping at the peripheral and not the core of his insights. What makes sense, though, is their concern that Popper's words and ideas be read carefully and from the texts he has written, rather than from second-hand rumours about his positivism or dogmatic demarcation of science from non-science, for example. They all help us appreciate the richness of his thought and his focus on rationality rather than certainty when applied to our knowledge claims and their acceptance or rejection by others. I find problems with any hero worship because it reminds me of the romantic story of Pygmalion who fell in love with his own creation (and, as Greek mythology has it, was granted marriage to the miraculously born virgin by Aphrodite), so that the critical distance we expect of authors and artists (as a self-critical dimension of their process of creation) gets lost. Instead of following this tendency, I will try to expose the fruitful disagreements and shortcomings in Popper's thought so as to assess the merit and value of his legacy, and a legacy it indeed is.

I outline here the three major ways in which Popper and his ideas have been received and reviewed in the intellectual community in order to explain the ways in which I shall move between these views and try to set a fourth way of approaching his thought. I take it for granted that Popper contributed immensely to the intellectual world of the past century. I also think that his thought was cast widely enough to touch thinkers in different disciplines outside philosophy proper. Similarly, it might be of value to rethink his contributions and recast them in the appropriate postmodern mould they fit rather than leave them to the confines of analytic philosophy, conservative think-tanks, or critical rationalism alone. In fact, my intent is to use Popper as a bridge between various schools of thought and traditions, as he was a European who lived in Austria, New Zealand and the United Kingdom. Finally, the Popperian legacy underlined here brings his views much closer to some versions of Marxism and feminism as well as postmodernism, despite some of his own less popular ideas of a "Third World" (Popper [1972] 1979), which I ignore here.

Most commentators think of Popper and his intellectual legacy primarily in terms of his philosophy of science, while some recall his political philosophy. In what follows, I wish to twist the story a bit and present the legacy of an interesting set of ideas that informed the past century and still influences us today. My twist would be in foregrounding Popper's political and economic ideas and relating them to his methodology of science, showing along the way the ideological convictions they provide (similar to Shearmur's 1996 work, but different in approach). It is clear from the historical record that the particular political circumstances under which European intellectuals laboured were such that one either tried to escape or engage them. For instance, the Vienna Circle's method of analysing language and ideas, trying to rid our communication from any metaphysical overlays, was one way to escape the political elements associated with or underlying human interaction. This way, the "scientific" approach to culture, could reduce all the ideological noise to clear and concise modes of communication: objectivity, value-neutrality, precision, verification and rationality are the modernist hallmarks of the period between the two world wars. By the time fascism swept the European landscape, clarity in communication was an odd intellectual obsession that seemed not to have any practical application unless one worked for one of the many propaganda machines. The escape routes for intellectuals became fairly narrow (if they existed at all), especially if one were a Jew. Should one run from one's homeland (as Popper did to New Zealand), or should one engage the regime, criticize it, and fight till the bitter end?

It is within this political context that Popper, too, shifted his interest from science to politics, from abstract methodological

7

ideas (about falsification instead of verification) to harsh indictments of ideas as such and those who profess them (Plato and Hegel and Marx, for example). Popper saw in certain ideas and movements a threat to freedom and individuality, to autonomy and creativity. The Soviet communists and the Nazi Party made it very clear that there is a short distance between ideology and the gulags or gas chambers. But Popper's critical approach was neither based on the political rhetoric of his day nor on its misguided application (in the Soviet Union, for example); instead his critique reverted to his philosophy of science as a means by which to discredit a shaky methodology. He seems to be telling us: go to the source! Find the foundation on which a theory or ideology or political model rests, and see how sound it indeed is.

The story I wish to retell here details the primacy of Popper's ideological convictions as a springboard to understanding his revolutionary impact on the late twentieth century and the dawn of this century, rather than one focused on his biography (see, for example, Hacohen 2000) or his academic disputes (see, for example, the popularized *Wittgenstein's Poker*, Edmonds & Eidinow 2001). I guess one way of spinning Popper's tale is to remind ourselves that in the postmodern culture that is more open to alternative ideas and less concerned with any foundation whatsoever, Popper provides a moral option if not a middle ground: at once a staunch rationalist (with some of the modernist trappings this entails) and yet a libertarian anarchist (with some of the individualistic trappings of relativism, solipsism, and selfishness). The ghosts of World War II and the Cold War are no longer with us: we are not frightened by fascist institutions with military power, but rather by terrorist organizations that traverse national boundaries and are therefore less predictable in their political and militant manifestations. And this affects the way we think and the topics we choose to study and research. So, instead of reviewing Popper's legacy in a vacuum, I wish to emphasize the context that gave rise to it, and that has been nurtured by those looking for legitimation for their ideas and practices.

The brief commentary on Popper's views, their critical assessments, and some of the revisions that they have undergone with a second generation of Popperians, offers an opportunity to re-examine how fractured and ideologically loaded his ideas continue to be, given the postmodern environment in which ideas and theories, principles and values are being used and abused, recycled and reinvented. I am interested in reading some of his influences backwards, so to speak, so as to see who and for what reasons would justify their own views based on the prestige Popper's ideas have gained over the years. It is in this sense that my critical review is neither biographical nor scholarly in the traditional sense. It is rather a cultural critique that incorporates all the relevant elements in Popper's life and writings, the circumstances under which some books and essays were rejected or well received, without being an apologist or a disciple.

In closing these prefatory remarks, I would like to mention my own so-called intellectual odyssey because I return repeatedly to the same texts and authors to find insights and hints with which to bolster my own arguments and pleas. Cultural critics of science follow in one form or another the debates of the Vienna Circle, the developments of science in the twentieth century (from the theory of relativity to quantum mechanics and beyond), and the ensuing critiques of science that were both internal (methodologists from Popper to Kuhn and Feyerabend) and external to its community (sociologists of science from Merton to the Edinburgh Strong Program and social epistemologists, and feminists from Keller to Harding and Haraway, not to mention Marxists from the Frankfurt School to their American counterparts). Besides, is it not a prerequisite nowadays to be "reflexive" and explain why one is interested in this rather than that particular problem?

My personal note may explain why the present attempt to shift from the constraints of logic to those of a broader appeal to one's culture makes sense at all. I studied with one of Popper's disciples at Boston (Agassi) and was impressed with the radicalism of his position: Popper was an anti-inductivist in an age when (probabilistic) inductivism was the rage (from the Vienna Circle to its American stronghold in the guise of Hempel and Reichenbach); he was misunderstood and mocked more often than taken seriously; and he gave his students a bad reputation (some claim that for years they were unable to secure research grants). The Popperian critical edge and the dismissal of the view that Truth can ever be attained fit quite easily with my study of Marx and Marxism as well as developmental economics.

This odd couple – Marx and Popper – had a similar distrusting orientation toward the intellectual establishment of their day, and they both suffered ridicule and admiration in their respective cultures. They were, in a word, outsiders working inside a fully formulated intellectual framework, appreciating all along that the binary opposition between the outside and the inside is itself problematic and invites challenges. I know that Popper criticized Marx's theory as unscientific, but that says more about Popper's obsession with the problem of demarcation (of science from non-science) than about the presumed incommensurability of the alleged scientific models proposed by Marx and Popper. Regardless of their differences (and there are indeed too many to enumerate here), they exemplify a similar critical and sceptical attitude toward knowledge claims, while attempting to replace one scientific theory with a "better" one. Of course each has his own criteria according to which scientific credibility ought to be granted, but they both still remain committed to nature's "reality" (and in this sense they remain realists), to the empirical verification or refutation of theories, and to some criterion of intersubjectivity as the basis for proposing general statements. In other words, neither broke completely with modern (philosophy of) science.

By the time I was synthesizing and applying a Marxist–Popperian critique of economics and medicine, I realized that even these radical thinkers may not be radical enough. That is, their views have a tendency to calcify and become as dogmatic as those they originally challenged and criticized. I have to admit that this sort of "consensus-building" orthodoxy is probably more characteristic of the followers of Marx and Popper than of the actual written books and essays of these thinkers themselves, but because I was studying with the followers of these thinkers, I still craved something more radical. The next step in this intellectual journey was postmodernism.

Working on science and technology from a postmodern perspective was exciting and problematic. In fact, certain views of realism and certain commitments to empiricism had to be suspended (but not completely given up) in order to render full play to ideas about the construction of knowledge claims and the fictional character of our historical records (namely, the appreciation that narratives exaggerate the facts or present them from a particular perspective with certain built-in limitations). Having read some feminist critiques and the works of some sociologists of science, I lost all interest in whatever Popper and his disciples had for their critical rationality. And then I read Donna Haraway's work. Although I understand that I walked into the middle of her conversation with some feminist epistemologists and some other radical socialist feminists, I found myself suffering from an intellectual vertigo. It is not that Haraway uses the term "situated knowledge" that brought back memories of Popper's terminology, but rather that she insists on retaining certain commitments that I had long given up on because they were associated in my mind with Popper and the Vienna Circle. In short, Haraway sent me back to Popper!

And the more I became acquainted with postmodernism, especially through Jean-François Lyotard's works, the more I realized that there were wonderful tools with which to tackle the problems postmodernism was interested in solving (and that resembled, on some level, those of Marx and Popper). It was the putative status of truth, the ongoing quest for a better formulation of conjectures and hypotheses (rather than pursuing closure in the name of a specific solution), the plurality of ideas and methods of inquiry, an absolute insistence on individual freedom and responsibility, and the struggle with a moral grounding that would be contextual rather than rigid and foundational. Popper could offer his own ideas as a starting point, if anyone outside his circle of admirers ever bothered to read his works. It is with this in mind that I offer my own critical assessment, full of respect and dissent, not to what has become of Popper, but to some of the epistemic commitments and moral convictions that he professed at a time when they were not so popular. So, the courage to propose ideas and solutions to social and political problems illustrates a certain intellectual courage we can all learn from.

CHAPTER I

CHAPTER I
The open society as liberty

Four main concerns inform this chapter: first, to provide a brief summary of some of the main ideas attributed to Popper related to social science and politics and their reception over the past century; secondly, to rehearse some of the standard critiques of his work, so as to emphasize how someone from the margins of philosophy, someone commonly associated with the Vienna Circle, was eventually taken seriously by the philosophical establishment and appreciated on all fronts; thirdly, to illustrate the relevance of his ideas about politics and freedom to the increased popularity of his ideas about scientific methodology; and fourthly, to assess his critical rationalism as an ideology and guide for political leadership and institutions.

A brief survey

The Open Society and Its Enemies (Popper [1943] 1966) became an event more than just a book published during World War II. What made this two-volume book such a sensation was its clear line of demarcation, a methodological device Popper has used so effectively in his discussion of the philosophy of science. Epictetus did the same: let us divide the world and life, he said, into those things that are within our control and those which are not; the trick is, of course, figuring out what events and issues fall into either category. In a brilliant move, Epictetus provides us with a road map, a scale and a benchmark, while shifting the responsibility to us to decide which items or events belong to which category. It seems simple at first, every student can understand the line of demarcation, but it becomes a difficult task, as all students realize halfway into the reading, when it is up to them to decide whether being students taking a philosophy course is or is not within their control (so that whatever grade they receive should or should not be within your control, too). Once students wake up in the middle of the process, the tables have turned on them, so to speak, so any climate of victimhood is obviously inappropriate: is this within your control or not? How would you know ahead of time? How do you approach your life's decision within this matrix?

Popper uses the same device: all societies are divided into two kinds – closed and open. Here are the lines of demarcation, here are the criteria according to which one decides which society belongs in which camp, and it is now up to us to apply the criteria and figure out which societies are more open or less, and then expect different things to occur within each one of them. The burden, so to speak, is put squarely on the shoulders of the assessors, so that the self-proclamations of the heads of state or political leaders are discounted from the start. But in order to set up this theoretical framework, Popper offers us the history of philosophy, just as anyone since Hegel has done. The use of history, we all agree, is a tricky undertaking, since one can be selective and thereby manipulative in doing so. Is this necessarily incorrect? Probably yes, if one believes that history provides a uniform and incontestable narrative that is absolutely true; probably no, if one is aware, since the nineteenth century, that narratives are made by people who have agendas and their own perspectives (consciously or subconsciously) so that they might make different choices to support their views.

Where does Popper rest? Surely he is guilty of choosing what fits his theoretical framework. So, now we have a choice to make. Either we can study the framework and appreciate its potential usefulness or we can analyse the examples he uses to bolster or support this framework, and, if found wanting, discard the entire framework. Some scholars have chosen the former strategy, others the latter. Some have argued that since Popper is not an expert in the history of ideas, anything he says about Socrates and Plato, Hegel and Marx should be doubted and ignored. Others have said that even although Popper might be wrong in this or that interpretation of the texts, his overall view is of interest and should be considered for its own merit. Why, then, use the historical record to begin with? There is something about the European upbringing and tradition that compels intellectuals to pay homage to their elders, pay tribute to their forefathers (even if they disagree with them), and acknowledge that one's own ideas have a history and as such rely on the ideas of others. So, there is a difference between gesturing to the icons of the history of ideas, misusing their words to fit one's own, or finding nuggets of wisdom in what they said as illustrations for what is currently problematic and symptomatic of one's culture and its ailments.

Writing, as he did, during World War II, in exile (New Zealand), and outside the machinery that opposed the forces of fascism in Europe, probably was the best Popper could do for the war effort, so to speak. One can raise a sword, a gun, or a pen; obviously the pen seems powerless against the sword and the gun, as Stalin is reputed to have claimed when he challenged the Pope's position in regards to dictating treaties to end the war (how many divisions does he have under his control?). But Popper's pen, in a manner of speaking, turned out to be quite powerful, after all. As he says in the Preface, written in 1950:

> Although much of what is contained in this book took shape at an earlier date, the final decision to write it was made in March 1938, on the day I received the news of the invasion of Austria. The writing extended into 1943. ([1943] 1966, viii)

Popper admits that this was an emotional undertaking, one that took on a "harsher" tone and critical approach just because the times were emotional. One had to stand tall and face fascism in the manner it had never been faced before; eventually, one had to face communism of the Soviet kind in a likewise manner, as reports of the gulags were forthcoming, and the massacres of millions of citizens under the Soviet rule were compared to the atrocities of the Nazis. One had to answer the questions, Is your own society "open" or "closed"? How would you know? Under what conditions can you make the assessment? Perhaps a bit of history could help; perhaps historical records could be culled so as to bring about a reassessment of the political conditions of the twentieth century. Socrates was a democrat, Plato was not! Socrates believed

15

in the intrinsic value of an open-ended dialogue, where the truth remained as elusive as the next argumentative move. Plato believed in a blueprint of a state, where everyone knew his or her role and position, where you could prefigure where and why you belonged in what social group or class; all you had to do is know your proper place. It is in this sense, then, that this society is closed. I shall refrain from analysing the details of Popper's scholarship concerning ancient Greek philosophy in general and his textual analysis of Socrates and Plato in particular. Suffice here to say that it's a useful cognitive device to claim a distinction between the two so as to illustrate some concerns Popper has with his contemporary culture.

Popper explains already in his Introduction to *The Open Society and Its Enemies* that his distinction between the open and closed society is one related to the history of civilization, so that his own contribution

> attempts to show that this civilization has not yet fully recovered from the shock of its birth – the transition from the tribal or "closed society", with its submission to magical forces, to the "open society" which sets free the critical powers of man.
>
> (*Ibid.*: 1)

And in order to illustrate the shift from one to the other, it also answers the question raised above about the conditions under which such a transformation would be possible:

> It analyses the principles of democratic social reconstruction, the principles of what I may term "piecemeal social engineering" in opposition to "Utopian social engineering" . . . (*Ibid.*)

It is in these opening passages that Popper already alludes to his *The Poverty of Historicism* (1957) where he argues forcefully about the misapplication of the scientific method to the social sciences in general and to political institutions in particular. As he explains, there is a distinction between *scientific prediction* and *historical prophecy*, and when political philosophers or leaders confuse the two, they become guilty of closing the society to any future re-examination or reconstruction.

16

In *The Poverty of Historicism*, Popper provides a set of arguments that connect and distinguish between the method used in the natural sciences and the one used in the social sciences. Clearly, one aim of such an exercise is to set a line of demarcation between science and non-science. But in addition, this kind of approach also alerts us to the inapplicability of one method whose effectiveness in physics, for example, remains indisputable (in terms of theoretical breakthroughs illustrated over the historical record as well as useful applications over time) when applied to the social sciences. In going about his survey, Popper terms historicists all those who advocate the view that historical prediction is the principal aim of the social sciences (1957: 3). Obviously, there are differences between the laws of nature, as they are called, because of their absolute uniformities, regardless of geographical and demographic differences, while the "laws of social life" depend to a large extent on historical conditions and the particular situations under which we live (*Ibid.*: 5).

Popper suggests the criteria according to which one can distinguish or realize the difference between one set of laws and the other, the ones associated with physical as opposed to social laws. They include generalization, experimentation, novelty, complexity, inexactitude of prediction, objectivity and valuation, holism, intuitive understanding, quantitative methods and essentialism versus nominalism (Chapter 1). Instead of following all the details of these features and their related characteristics when applied to either set of laws, let me briefly offer the main line of argument that is threaded through them.

Unlike astrophysicists who can construct a model of celestial movement to explain their observations and then predict, with a great deal of precision, the movement or appearance of a particular planet in the future, social scientists find themselves observing, explaining and predicting future events in a manner that influences their pronouncements: theirs turn out to be self-fulfilling prophecies. Referring to ancient myths and narratives, Popper has this to say:

> The idea that a prediction may have influence upon the predicted event is a very old one. Oedipus, in the legend, killed his father whom he had never seen before; and this was the direct result of the prophecy which has caused his father to abandon

> him. This is why I suggest the name "*Oedipus effect*" for the influence of the prediction upon the predicted event (or, more generally, for the influence of an item of information upon the situation to which the information refers), whether this influence tends to bring about the predicted event, or whether it tends to prevent it. (*Ibid.*: 13)

Sure enough, Popper continues his psychological journey into historical legends so as to remind us not so much about Oedipus's love for his mother, as a son and protector, as a sexual perversity or fantasy, but about the influence that a prediction has on those listening to it. Although there is some "indeterminacy" in the physical sciences (*Ibid.*: 14), an observer cannot "cause" a physical event to take place, or prevent it from doing so, in the sense that one can and often does interfere in the social sciences when public announcements about war or famine, inflation or food shortage do indeed accelerate or retard these prophecies from taking shape. Moreover, one can compare the social sciences to biological science where mutual influence among the variables *necessitates* a holistic approach, one that can appreciate evolution, for example, as a process that combines variables not simply reduced to individual, causal relations, so that historicism is akin to an "organic theory" rather than a physical theory (*Ibid.*: 17–19). When social life is studied under these circumstances and is explained in this manner, one must also appreciate the notion of "tacit knowledge" popularized by Michael Polanyi (1958) that is prevalent in societies, a way to appreciate social trends and behaviour that are not reduced to causal elements and processes one can deconstruct after the events have occurred.

Popper distinguishes between two kinds of predictions, those "about an event which we can do nothing to prevent. I shall call such a prediction a '*prophecy*' . . . [*T*]*echnological* predictions . . . form a basis of *engineering*. They are, so to speak, constructive, intimating the steps open to us *if* we want to achieve certain results" (1957: 43). This distinction is what forms the basis of his distinction between open and closed societies (as we shall see below). But the distinction is not as strict or clear-cut, after all. As Popper admits: "All social engineering, no matter how much it prides itself on its realism and on its scientific character, is doomed to remain a Utopian dream" (*Ibid.*: 47). As far as he is concerned, social reality as seen historically never complies with a rational construction, a plan or an agenda, Platonic or otherwise. Instead, there are conflicts and specific situations that come about in a manner that disrupts and changes any idea or plan, no matter how rational. In making this argument, Popper criticizes Plato's notion of "a powerful philosopher-king who would put into practice some carefully thought out plans" as a fairy-tale as well as its so-called democratic equivalent fuelled by the "superstition that enough people of good will may be persuaded by rational argument to take planned action" (*Ibid.*). By contrast, he suggests, "Social midwifery [Socrates' method] is the only perfectly reasonable activity open to us, the only activity that can be based upon scientific foresight" (*Ibid.*: 49). And the scientific insight and foresight that are relevant to the social sciences, turn out to be the method of trial and error, the method that encourages rational criticism, the kind that exposes mistakes and allows us to make the kind of theoretical and practical changes from which we can learn for future reference (*Ibid.*: 57).

Popper's recommendation for the social sciences is to maintain the bare minimum of reference to the natural sciences in methodological terms. Since a methodology that claims explanatory and predictive powers as precise and universal as those found in the history of science is untenable, Popper switches to a technological approach to sociology and the other social sciences. When recommending piecemeal engineering, piecemeal technology and social technology as methods and approaches to the seeming complexity of social phenomena, Popper warns against "scientism", a phrase he attributes to his colleague Hayek, which is a "dogmatic methodological naturalism", so reductive and unrealistic that it undermines the credibility and even beauty found in the natural sciences and the methods they employ (*Ibid.*: 60). The "misguided effort to copy these methods" (*Ibid.*: 105), is fundamentally bound to undermine any potential success that could be associated with the social sciences. But even piecemeal engineering as a method is problematic, as Popper confesses in one of his notes. Once again, he attributes to Hayek the insight that even in engineering one must see the entire theoretical framework to make minor changes, and that all the relevant details are interconnected in multiple ways, that simply focusing on one area or one detail is bound to be a mistake (*Ibid.*: 64). Popper's rejoinder is of interest here: "The piecemeal technologist or engineer recognizes that *only a minority of social institutions are consciously designed while the vast majority have just 'grown', as the undersigned results of human actions*" (*Ibid.*: 65). Obviously, most institutions, even when not formally designed, have some functional purpose that corresponds to human needs and wants, and that thereby can be rationally examined. If they had no function whatsoever, these institutions would wither away in a quasi-Darwinian manner, and not make it into the next evolutionary step of their existence.

Socrates and Plato are never too far from Popper's analysis:

> The piecemeal engineer knows, like Socrates, how little he knows. He knows that we can learn only from our mistakes. Accordingly, he will make his way, step by step, carefully comparing the results expected with the results achieved, and always on the look-out for the unavoidable unwanted consequences of any reform; and he will avoid undertaking reforms of a complexity and scope which make it impossible for him to disentangle causes and effects, and to know what he is really doing. (*Ibid.*: 67)

Socrates, who was told by Chaerephon that the oracle of Delphi told him that no one was wiser than Socrates, claimed that his unpopularity was not due to this pronouncement alone, but that indeed it was based simply on the fact that he didn't think he knew what he didn't know (a minimalist definition of knowledge and wisdom, rather than an expansive one about the accumulation of facts; see *Apology*: 21, Plato). And here he is, not the midwife of ideas, but the seeker of truth who has no prefigured set of ideas or planned society. Popper's preferred method of trial and error, of small changes and reforms that themselves are prone to be misguided but easily corrected, is revisited with Socrates in mind. It is in this sense, then, that Popper explains the difference between the historicist utopian vision and prophecy and his own piecemeal engineering as something that "in practice, [turns out] to be a difference not so much in scale and scope as in caution and preparedness for unavoidable surprises" (1957: 69). This is the same difference one finds between the holist and the piecemeal engineer, "while the piecemeal engineer can attack his problem with an open mind as to the scope of the reform, the holist cannot do this; for he has decided beforehand that a complete reconstruction is possible and necessary" (*Ibid.*). One can detect here the eventual criticism Popper levels against both Hegel and Marx, albeit in their respective contexts and for different textual and intellectual details. This is how Popper concludes his remarks:

> This, we may say, is the central mistake of historicism. Its *"laws of development" turn out to be absolute trends;* trends which, like laws, do not depend on initial conditions, and which carry us irresistibly in a certain direction into the future. They are the basis of unconditional *prophecies*, as opposed to conditional scientific *predictions*.   (*Ibid.*: 128)

The social sciences cannot formulate theories and models that have the same status as those of the natural sciences. They will always fall short for three reasons: first, they remain historically contextualized, and therefore limited in their universal appeal even when they claim the contrary; secondly, they are holistic and utopian, and therefore prefigure that which still needs to be figured out, lacking an openness to changes and modifications; and thirdly, they are bound to influence what they claim to predict, and therefore do not describe causal relations but participate in causing certain events to happen. Put differently, scientific predictions, including those of scientific engineers, are deducible from theories or general statements plus initial conditions according to which they are formulated, whereas prophecies, including those made within the historicist framework, are not deducible in this manner, because so-called laws of history are not empirical generalizations from observable facts, so to speak, but are revealed laws of trends and propensities. As we shall see in later chapters, the appeal to science (and not to scientism) has had specific attraction in the past century and into the present because of the prestigious status associated with technoscience.

It is also noteworthy that Popper, like some of his predecessors in the history of ideas, illustrates how his "philosophy" is of one cloth, so to speak: the framework he constructs should provide the intellectual and methodological scaffolding for all the areas of research to which he devotes his energy and with which his readers and students are concerned. Just as Kant moved from the critique of "pure reason" to morality and aesthetics, so does Popper move from the philosophy and methodology and history of science to political philosophy.

What distinguishes Popper from any other philosopher of science of the twentieth century is his close emotional attachment to his arguments. As he admits in *The Open Society and Its Enemies*, "The systematic analysis of historicism aims at something like scientific status. This book does not. Many of the opinions expressed are personal. What it owes to scientific method is largely the awareness of its limitations" ([1943] 1966: 3). But Popper does not simply confess his own emotional state of mind; he goes on to impute "motives" to his interlocutors or to those guilty of having propounded something akin to a historicist position. He uses terms such as "deeper motives" when describing the prophets who "may give expression to a deep-seated feeling of dissatisfaction", and later claims that "their dreams may indeed give hope and encouragement to some who can hardly do without them" (*Ibid.*: 4). He labels his intellectual opponents as "disappointed historicists" who have a certain "attitude" (*Ibid.*: 5). If one were to forget who the author is, one would be tempted to think of Popper's fellow Viennese, Sigmund Freud or Alfred Adler or any other psychologist. The clear-cut arguments of the past, accompanied as they are by historical evidence, should stand on their own; is not this what Aristotle suggested when he admonished us to separate the argument from the person who makes it (*ad hominem*)?

When we keep in mind the fact that Popper is fighting the good fight against fascism and against the totalitarian regime of the Soviet Union, he might be forgiven for some of the more strongly phrased assertions he makes. For example: "Only democracy provides an institutional framework that permits reform without violence, and so the use of reason in political matters" (*Ibid.*: 4). This may be true. This may be true in light of Kant's political writings as well; yet, it's accompanied in the next sentence by the following emotive language once again: "A further motive, it seems, can be found if we consider that historicist metaphysics are apt to relieve men from the strain of their responsibilities" (*Ibid.*). Here we see how the two concerns are linked. Reason is the foundation for reforms, and reforms can take place only under certain conditions that encourage them, that are open to them. Moreover, those who commit to these reforms and use their reason also acknowledge that they are the ones responsible for the ideas that lead to these reforms, and for their implementation. If there are problems associated with either the reforms or their implementations, then there is room for correction, for change. If something goes terribly wrong, it is we who are responsible for our actions, not some demigod or an emperor.

Popper the critical thinker is aware of how he might come across in this loaded text, so he is quick to say that "What I am going to say here is therefore not meant as a dogmatic assertion, however boldly I may perhaps sometimes express my opinions" (*Ibid*.: 171). Strategically, this is pure Popper: conjectures and refutations! Express your views as boldly as possible, as clearly as possible, with as few qualifications as possible, and thereby set them up for easy and full critical assessment. Don't hide behind dependent clauses that confuse the meaning you wish to give your words; don't use metaphors when simple prose will do.

As Popper reminds his readers, "the magical or collectivist society will be also called the *closed society*, and the society in which individuals are confronted with personal decisions, the *open society*" (*Ibid*.: 173). By magical, he means the kind of society that is driven by tradition and taboos, a society that might change its customs and habits but only if by magical inspiration, as if instructed by the gods. What makes it collectivist is the fact that the group or tribe is more important than its members, and therefore what is good for all must necessarily be good for the individual. By contrast, Popper would like to see more "rational reflection" and individual decision-making, such that changes would be discussed and analysed, tried out and revised once again, until the collection of individuals comes up with policies and decision that might fit the society as a whole. The openness, then, is to every mode of criticism, to any personal voice, no matter how meek, no matter how low. Looking back at the ancient Greeks, Popper already sees hints of the shift from the closed to the open society: "The new faith of the open society, the faith in man, in equalitarian justice, and in human reason, was perhaps beginning to take shape, but it was

23

not yet formulated" (*Ibid.*: 189). The shift is seen by Popper in the switch from teacher to student, from mentor to disciple, as in the case of Socrates and Plato. Connecting Plato's view of the soul, he says:

> That Plato, with his longing for unity and harmony, visualized the structure of the human soul as analogous to that of a class-divided society shows how deeply he must have suffered. Plato's greatest conflict arises from the deep impression made upon him by the example of Socrates, but his own oligarchic inclinations strive only too successfully against it. In the field of rational argument, the struggle is conducted by using the argument of Socrates' humanitarianism against itself.
>
> (*Ibid.*: 197)

Once again, Plato's own inner struggle is surmised here; once again, Plato's failure to succeed his teacher is understood in terms of personal inclinations, certain deep-seated fears that only a good therapy session could bring forth and relieve. But is it really a struggle between Socrates' views and those of Plato? Is there truth in Popper's assessment? Or are the two used so as to remind us of the inevitable conflict or incompatibility between a view of social order and political institutions that promotes stability by appealing to tradition and one that is willing to risk some upheavals and changes in the name of human reason and responsibility?

Popper ends the first volume of *The Open Society and Its Enemies* with some lines that could have come out of any utopian text, and of the texts he opposes as overly constructive and closed:

> Our dream of heaven cannot be realized on earth. Once we begin to rely upon our reason, and to use our powers of criticism, once we feel the call of personal responsibilities, and with it, the responsibility of helping to advance knowledge, we cannot return to a state of internal submission to tribal magic. For those who have eaten of the tree of knowledge, paradise is lost. (*Ibid.*: 200)

These words could have been written by Plato, Hegel, or Marx, the three thinkers criticized by Popper most strongly in this text.

They sound messianic, prophetic, and definitely biblical. The allusions to human destiny and its transformation, the allusion to the tree of knowledge in the Garden of Eden, is something of a surprise for the critical rationalist whose views we are elucidating here. The emotive language with which he approaches his subject matter and his subjects is now transformed into the language of an oracle – but an oracle with distinct accent, one that eschews the temptation of psychologizing everyone and everything so as to find empirical data that can be rationally formulated.

Popper's love–hate relationship with Marx permeates many passages in both *The Poverty of Historicism* and *The Open Society and Its Enemies*. Not only does he give Marx credit for the very title of his work (the *Poverty* . . . as opposed to the *Open Society* borrowed from Henri Bergson), but he also finds in him much worthy of study, respect, and therefore critical assessment. This, indeed, is an important feature in Popper's philosophy that might be hidden or taken for granted: criticism is levelled at worthy opponents and ideas, while others fall by the wayside. We learn from mistakes and build upon them, rather than discard or ignore them. It is in this light that I suggest we read Popper's criticism of Marx. Much has been said in the past few decades about how hostile Popper is to Marx and how misinformed his reading of Marx remains. First, I think that agreeing or disagreeing with an author is no indication of disrespect or intentional misreading. Secondly, as any good reader knows, we bring to the text our own biases and find in it what we are looking for; in this sense, there is never an absolutely correct reading of a text. And thirdly, Popper's venom against the totalitarian regime of the Soviet Union has been confused by many (including him) with Marx's ideas and theories; this confusion is unfortunate and quite beside the point. Anyone can claim the authority of a theory or a principle and appeal to either for legitimacy, but this has nothing to do with the actual application or misapplication of said theory or principle. This is true in personal relationships, in religious matters, and definitely in political affairs.

Popper aligns himself with Marx's "opposition to psychologism", namely the doctrine that "all laws of social life must be ultimately reducible to the psychological laws of 'human nature'". He quotes Marx's epigram: "It is not the consciousness of man that determines

25

his existence – rather, it is his social existence that determines his consciousness" ([1943] 1966: II, 89). In this context, Popper wishes to highlight that the material conditions which were paramount in Marx's analysis are the ones that influence one's personality, one's psychological makeup. Here, Popper not only follows a methodological trail that might be informative for his own philosophy of science, but is anxious to set aside the inappropriate application of the scientific method to social matters. If there is a "scientific" element in the study of social life it should be confined to empirical data collection and observation.

Since Marx focused most of his attention on economics, or more precisely political economy, we find Popper paying homage to him in this direction. Although still concerned with the utopian inclinations of Marx, and therefore a target for Popper's critical evaluation (alongside Plato and Hegel), he does follow Marx's view on economics:

> Only pseudo-economics can seek to offer a background for rational economic planning. Truly scientific economics can merely help to reveal the driving forces of economic development through different historical periods . . . Its ultimate aim can only be "to lay bare the economic law of motion of human society" (Marx). (1957: 49)

I shall return to some of the relevant ideas of Popper regarding economic thought and the methodology that best emulates his scientific method in a later chapter. Here I wish to explain the extent to which Popper's rejection of holism (and as such collectivism, which he found to be more dangerous as legitimating policies) and utopian thinking, as mistaken methods and principles of inquiry, shift more specifically to certain studies of human life and social institutions.

The problem for the social sciences is whether the ultimate category of analysis is society or the individual, regardless of an entire other discussion as to which came first. For Plato, Hegel and Marx, society comes logically and methodologically prior to the individual (if not chronologically), while for Popper (like Mill) the opposite is the case. There is a "superiority of society over the individual" ([1943] 1966: II, 99) that undermines the study of the psychologically rational behaviour of individuals. Popper's objection to this view translates into his view of a situational logic of human and social behaviour that is unique to the social sciences and that differs radically from the natural sciences – it therefore requires a different method of enquiry (*Ibid.*: 97). I shall elaborate more on this in Chapter 3.

If Marx's views are read exclusively in terms of (a) society being the unit of historical and empirical analysis and (b) a messianic dream of a communist utopia, then Popper can find much fault with them. Obviously, individuals make up a society and it's up to them, however they organize themselves, to change it if it is found lacking in any manner. Likewise, any messianic vision promises too much and may be used as an inducement for revolutionary changes whose unintended consequences can be detrimental to the original intentions in whose name they were undertaken. However, if Marx's views are read as (a) an attempt to study the forces of political economy historically, (b) an attempt to critically revise Hegel's idealism and put it on its head, so to speak, (c) an attempt to add empirical lustre to philosophical speculations, (d) an attempt to deconstruct classical economic thought with a keen eye on the methods it used, and (e) a theory open to future critical assessment because of its predictions, then Marx comes closer to Popper's own ideals. Let me explain some more in this regard.

I have always found it unproblematic to claim intellectual affinity to both Marx and Popper. In fact, the switching back and forth from their texts and ideas never bothered me emotionally – to use Popper's indictment against Plato's deep-seated frustration. On the contrary, Popper's terse, twentieth-century formulations made up for the convoluted, nineteenth-century phrasings of Marx. They both wish to reveal the truth about their subject matter; they both are students of the history of ideas, and wish to use it to promote their own views; they both like to demarcate between science and pseudo-science; and they both provide theoretical frameworks that are at once comprehensive, yet clear enough to allow criticism. Neither finds solace in irrational musings nor in fanciful dreams, although both are hopeful that their writings can eliminate suffering and bring about human freedom and happiness.

Critical reception

It is interesting to note that among his admiring critics Robert Ackermann, for example, makes the claim that "Popper has not, in any event, been a major figure in theoretical debates about social theory" (Ackermann 1976: 157), because he has failed to address specific issues in social affairs (unlike his contribution to the natural sciences). He goes on to say that there is interest in Popper's view concerning the social sciences, but this is because "he is one of the few philosophers of science to have explicitly argued a methodological scheme designed to have normative impact on both the physical and the social sciences" (*Ibid.*: 159). As a way of defending Popper from the charge that he is merely a positivist looking for facts where other elements come to light in the study of social life, Ackermann explains that Popper's concern with facts might be different from his concern with a "justificationist" testing of theories, so that he is much more of a social theorist than meets the eye (*Ibid.*: 161). What makes Popper a social scientist in this sense is his overarching methodology, one that, if correct, is equally applicable to all areas of study. Facts, for Popper the realist, are captured in observation statements and those are useful, in turn, when (a) applied to hypotheses as cases for falsifying this or that general or universal claim, (b) as explicanda, as what we wish to understand, and (c) as situations and conditions for technology to apply to. This procedure would be useful for either the social or the natural sciences.

Bryan Magee, known as much as a British politician as he is an academic, explains the distinction Popper makes in his theories between the logic and history of science and the psychology of its practitioners (Magee 1973: 23–7). As he says, for Popper: "falsification in whole or in part is the anticipated fate of all hypotheses, and we should even rejoice in the falsification of a hypothesis that we have cherished as our brain-child" (*Ibid.*: 32). He also talks about corroboration of theories and their temporary preference by comparison to others (*Ibid.*: 34). As Magee suggests, it is incorrect to take Popper's falsification criterion of demarcation between science and non-science to be a demarcation between sense and nonsense. The reason this point is important, as far as Magee explains, is because it follows the positivists' concern with meaningful and meaningless statements, which Popper revisits from another angle. For Popper, general scientific laws cannot be verified like single statements, and therefore eschew the kind of analysis offered by the positivists; moreover, general metaphysical statements, however unverifiable, have been instrumental in informing science and scientific theories, and as such cannot be simply dismissed as meaningless (*Ibid.*: 40–41). And this would be the case for both social and natural science alike.

Magee makes the excellent point that Popper's philosophy is driven by problems that require solutions, however incomplete and erroneous. In this sense, then, Popper engages his subject matter as an existentialist, with the kind of authenticity that commits him to solve problems rather than figure out who said what about this or that subject matter. The focus shifts from intellectual leaders and their texts to intellectual and practical problems and their potential solutions (*Ibid.*: 61–3).

> The scientist and the artist, far from being engaged in opposed or incompatible activities, are both trying to extend our understanding of experience by the use of creative imagination subjected to critical control, and so both are using irrational as well as rational faculties. Both are exploring the unknown and trying to articulate the search and its findings. Both are seekers after truth who make indispensable use of intuition.
>
> (*Ibid.*: 64)

Magee appreciates the political nature of science and its uses in society to solve problems, so long as this is a society that encourages every citizen to critically engage everyone else and challenge the authority of the government. He agrees with Popper's idea to promote some regulations so that unbridled capitalism or freedom would not deteriorate into a "might makes right" situation, where no rules govern those intending to take advantage of those in weaker positions (*Ibid.*: 75–7). He insists on optimal (i.e. more may not be better, but a balance must be struck) and not absolute (i.e. more is always better) freedom, just as he appreciates, borrowing from Popper's own words, that the strength of fortresses is not sufficient to make them effective; "they have also to be properly manned" (*Ibid.*: 78).

He agrees that piecemeal engineering is an "unfortunate" and "pejorative" sounding term, being "heartless" (*Ibid.*: 104–5); but this is not the case, according to Magee, who emphasizes that there is a passion and concern that makes this method of implementing social changes a far better choice than a revolution in which many suffer and die for a cause unclear to all. There is a moral argument supporting this method, one that attempts to minimize suffering and cause the least harm (since it is done in small steps so that each misstep can be more quickly stopped or remedied).

Elsewhere, Magee seems to agree with Ackermann that because Popper's main concern with the social sciences in general and politics in particular were more methodological than anything else, his approach ends up having "limitations and shortcomings". "It is seldom that Popper's work offers much guidance with them [practical politicians]" (Magee in Jarvie & Pralong 1999: 156–7). This kind of critique is reminiscent of the critique of Kant whose own moral injunctions were always taken to be formal and not substantive, more categorical than particular. "What should I do now?" is commonly treated with, "Apply the principle and then you will know." In this way there is a great deal of similarity between the two: their greatest strength, formulating a method, is perceived as their greatest weakness, formulating *only* a method and not a full-blown laundry-list of things to do and to avoid, prescribing exactly what one ought to do.

Problem solving is exactly what is on Popper's agenda, as far as his sympathetic critics are concerned. This is no small matter, for it is different from simply following someone's ideas and adding minor revisions to them, or following a tradition and adding some references to it. And the problems are not limited to the natural sciences, but are more profoundly affecting the very ability to study them. For example, when Giordano Bruno is burnt at the stake in 1600 or when Galileo is put under house arrest in 1633, we are shifting attention from celestial movement and the observation of stars (eventually astrophysics) to the political power of the church and its authority over the study of anything that could be perceived as a threat to its authority. Given the political climate of Popper's day, how can anyone study science if one's freedom is curtailed? How can anyone propose new venues of research if there are no institutions that sanction such a study? Although some three hundred years later, similar webs of interlocking influences exist between the pristine search for truth and the threat such a search can pose to political authorities of the church or fascist governments.

In the Preface to their collection of essays honouring the fiftieth anniversary of Popper's *Open Society*, Ian Jarvie and Sandra Pralong point out the major problem Popper tries to solve in this two-volume text (*Open Society*): "Why is the attack on freedom and democracy so popular?" Popper's answer ends up being an indictment against the major intellectual leaders who over the centuries haven't spoken out against such attack (Jarvie & Pralong 1999: xii). It's from this perspective that it makes sense for Popper to have critically re-evaluated Plato, Hegel and Marx; it is not that they personally have undermined freedom and democracy as such, but that in their intellectual pursuits they have paid less attention to the potential of individuals to participate in setting the tone of their future than to their grandiose ideas of a perfect society where freedom would be guaranteed. In them he finds thinkers who promote utopian thinking, hopeful as it is, that ends up procedurally to be totalitarian, for it does not provide the conditions under which individuals are preserved their rights and freedoms and governments can be dismissed without violence.

Although Popper is concerned with ideas and problems and their solutions, he has learned from his own experience that obstacles may be found anywhere, not least of all in the leadership of institutions, whether academic or political. Freedom, *à la* Popper, in Jarvie and Pralong's hands, turns out to be "not a comfortable option for everybody. Above all it makes individuals responsible for choosing, and responsible for the consequences of their choices" (*Ibid.*: xiii). The issue is therefore twofold: on the one hand, there are leaders who wish to maintain control over their people and therefore discourage freedom, and on the other hand, there are people who wish to maintain their ignorance and mental servitude so as not to be responsible for their choices and have the anguish associated with making decisions whose consequences remain unknown when making these decisions. Hence, anti-democratic tendencies collide from the top and the bottom in an unholy alliance: who would imagine that individuals would willingly undermine their own freedom?

It seems that Jarvie and Pralong have captured Popper's view best when they suggest that his own critique against the utopian totalitarianism of the past century can be a useful tool at the dawn of the new century, a century that celebrates hyper-global-capitalism as the ultimate bastion for freedom and democracy:

> Popper's critique of dogmatism, authority, and the reign of virtue can also be turned against those who think that capitalism as such, and capitalism as untrammeled as possible, will bring us the best of all possible worlds. The claim is sheer dogmatism, and the implementation would involve the kind of large-scale social engineering Popper would criticize as Utopian.
>
> (*Ibid.*: xv)

Capitalism itself, although claimed to be the crowning achievement of the twentieth century in terms of personal choices and freedom, can be just as problematic as utopianism. Just as a revolution can bring about human prosperity and happiness, even freedom (as seen in the American colonies in the eighteenth century), so can capitalism bring about human prosperity and happiness. But in both cases one needs to guard against abuses and suffering, provide guidelines and procedures that would protect the weakest people and bridle the authority of the most powerful; only then can both deliver on their promises. Without these provisions both can deliver disastrous results and have the same effects as any totalitarian regime. As they say:

> One of the beauties of Popper's general philosophy was that it granted a central place to mistakes. Making mistakes is a principal mechanism of learning . . . Popper advocates in the Open Society a methodological individualism and a moral individualism . . . The primacy of the individual is, for him, entirely a moral and a methodological, not a scientific matter. Hence the underlying individualism of Adam Smith, and his invisible hand argument that individuals acting selfishly will produce the greatest wealth should not be read as meaning it will produce the best, or most moral, or most decent, or most tolerant society. If those values trump wealth, it is our

responsibility to create institutions that curb the deficiencies of wealth-generating institutions. (*Ibid.*: xvii)

The issue is morality, however defined. To think that procedures or grand schemes as such would provide the social mechanism and political platform for justice for the individual is mistaken if moral considerations are not deployed at every stage as litmus tests for them. The creation and accumulation of wealth can be promoted and justified if it in fact preserves a moral boundary for the actions and interactions of individuals; when it fails to do so, then it should be curtailed and redirected. This, incidentally, is where Popper parts way with some classical and neo-classical economists all the way to the Chicago school of the late twentieth century (more on this in Chapter 2).

Douglas Williams claims that political concerns were always paramount to Popper and his works, perhaps in a way similar to Marx who was concerned with scientific theories in terms of their political implication: "politics was a central focus of Popper's work from the beginning" (Williams 1989: 15). It is Marx who first suggested, in his critique of classical economics, that so-called scientific models and theories, although claiming value-neutrality and objectivity, in fact reveal the prejudices of their promoters, featuring the self-interest of their authors and producers. The fact that there is a personal element in science, that one's personal views influence and determine the character of a scientific theory or model, was a novel idea in the nineteenth century. We must recall that the scientific revolutions of the sixteenth and seventeenth centuries attempted to overcome this hurdle: the shift from superstition and personal biases to observation and experimentation open to public scrutiny, the shift from the divine views of the chosen elite (of priests and shamans) to the mundane views of the common observer of nature (anyone qualifies, as long as another, independent observer can replicate the observation or the experiment). Marx's critique is devastating, for it overshadows the promise of the scientific enterprise to be free from prejudice and open to public scrutiny.

Williams also emphasizes the affinity between Popper's philosophy and the pragmatism of Charles Sanders Peirce (54ff.). This point is relevant because for Williams, Popper's attitude of reason-ableness turns the strict sense of rationality from an individual-istic, intellectual genius-like characteristic (that may differ from one person to another) into a "social character of reasonableness" (quoted from Popper [1943] 1966: II, 225). It is here, too, that Popper distinguishes between the social nature of the Socratic dia-logue and the authoritarianism and "pseudo-rationalism" of *Plato* (*Ibid.*: 85). And this attitude towards knowledge as a social enter-prise rather than an individual pursuit was important to Popper as a way to avoid violence and find solutions to the social and polit-ical problems on moral grounds (*Ibid.*: 89).

There are critics who have engaged the letter and not the spirit of Popper's critique of Plato, Hegel and Marx. Although Levinson is among the first to have provided a detailed critique of Popper's interpretation of Plato, complaining in places how Popper has misread and misinterpreted the Greek texts (Levinson 1970), I shall confine my own survey to those critiques that focused on Marx, both Cornforth's and Magee's. The former is a defender of Marx, while the latter a defender of Popper's critique of Marx. I should hasten to note that any textual reading can be criti-cized in principle; we bring our own spectacles and intellectual commitments to a text; we infuse a reading with our prejudices and thereby ignore some elements while focusing on others. There is, indeed, no objective or neutral reading that is exact and interpretation-free. But what is of interest in Popper's critique of Marx is his great sympathy with some of his ideas and con-cerns, with his set-up of problems, such as poverty and human suffering, exploitation and alienation. But for him Marx remains an ideologue, a messianic prophet and utopian thinker rather than a scientist whose rational discourse provides a self-legitimation like all others working within the scientific enterprise (of the natural and the social sciences). It is in this sense, then, that those defending Popper's critique and those of his detractors commit two kinds of fallacies.

The first confusion has to do with Marx's own work that traverses between his empirical research and his close observations of the economic and political reality of his day (for example, the work day) on the one hand, and his hypothetical and predictive solutions and proposals. I shall follow the moral theorists and call this the Naturalistic Fallacy. The second confusion is between Marx's own words and the actions of those, like the Soviets, who have claimed to follow his texts (this misapplication I shall call the Soviet Fallacy). We should note that according to Popper, any falsification is a sign of scientificity. Any theory or statement or principle that lends itself to falsification, that is open enough to be shown as being mistaken, in fact brings us closer to the truth, since we know now for sure what the case is not.

Maurice Cornforth has provided the most extensive and detailed response to Popper's dismissal of Marxism as a scientific theory, and the inability to falsify it. According to Cornforth, Popper misunderstood Marx's ideas and his own attempt to make them as scientific as possible, and the fact that his theory hasn't been falsified to the satisfaction of Popper does not make it in itself unscientific; if anything, its scientific status remains, its putative truth remains, and what is missing are particular instances according to which the failure of the theory, its falsification, is still being formulated. But, as we recall, the main question is always, does a theory lend itself in principle to falsification? And not, has this or that theory or claim been already falsified? Moreover, to equate Marxism with Soviet communism is inappropriate, for the kind of dogmatic Statism deployed by the Soviet leadership under Lenin and Stalin, for example, has little to do with the ideals of Marx and his version of socialism (Cornforth 1968: Ch. 1). What has been missing from the Soviet model is the transition from feudalism through capitalism to communism. The capitalist stage, where the accumulation of wealth is essential, allows for its own transformation into the socialist or communist stage. It's only then that each citizen can provide to the society according to his ability and receive in return from society according to his needs. One should note that in contemporary western societies the ones that come closest to the Marxian ideals are those countries (Scandinavian states come to mind) whose welfare programmes have become so extensive that the major part of the government budgets go to support them. The Soviet failure can be attributed, among many other factors, to the failure to provide the level of need satisfaction commensurate with socialist ideals. Yes, the right to work was an important component; but the manufacturing of consumer goods was sacrificed for the manufacturing of industrial goods and

35

services and the development of an international military power. This is where the Soviet Fallacy is most clearly seen.

Bryan Magee reminds us, quite naturally, that it seems on the face of it that when rationality, logic and science are used in political matters, one would expect an orderly and organized society along totalitarian and authoritarian lines, where efficiency and productivity are planned and managed well, something along the lines of the former Soviet Union. Popper's insight is to reverse this misconception and show that the best use of rationality, logic and science is within a democracy, where incompatible ideas can find a place and be heard and examined, criticized and changed (Magee 1985: 79ff.). Coming from a former politician in the UK, this is an excellent point. The trajectory towards productivity and efficiency, which Adam Smith already alluded to in his notion of the division of labour that eventually found adherents in Taylorism and Fordism (where assembly lines become the focus of capitalist efficiency), has been supported by scientific methods and the use of logic and rationality. But that trajectory can also point towards democracy, where individual decision-makers find ways to interact rationally and allow critical engagement so as to avoid duplication and waste. Put differently, the deployment of science in the affairs of the state might most fruitfully be undertaken in the economic sphere with the kind of institutional protection provided by the legal and moral spheres (expressed in laws and regulations).

Magee also suggests that the standard critique of Marxism offered by Popper is indeed effective in so far as any "scientific prediction" offered by the Marxist theory has been false. First, we should examine if Marx's statements indeed shift from prophecies to predictions and, if they do, then they must be allowed to be falsified. Instances of falsification, Magee should admit, lend these predictions scientific status rather than turn them into useless ideological pronouncements. As examples, Magee rehearses the following situations where Marx was wrong or where his predictions were in error. I shall quote Magee first, and then respond to each of his points in turn:

According to the theory only fully developed Capitalist countries could go Communist ... but in fact, except for

Czechoslovakia, all the countries to have gone Communist have been pre-industrial . . .   (Magee 1985: 101–2)

Those countries that went "communist" did so by name and rule only, but in fact weren't communist in any Marxist sense of the term. They did make all the means of production public, and they abolished private property. But they still didn't have the financial reserves to provide everyone's needs; they couldn't provide a broad enough social and medical safety net to ensure the happiness of all. We must recall that the ideal which Marx envisioned stipulated "to everyone according to his needs"! To continue:

The revolution would have to be based on the industrial proletariat: but Mao Tse-tung, Ho Chi Minn and Fidel Castro explicitly rejected this and based successful revolutions on the peasantries . . .   (*Ibid.*: 101–2)

Once again, just because this or that leader decides to tap this or that group to bring about the revolution does nothing to invalidate the principle that the working class will be instrumental in bringing about a revolutionary change in the structure of the state.

There are elaborate reasons why the industrial proletariat must inevitably get poorer, more numerous, more class-conscious and more revolutionary: in fact, in all industrial countries since Marx's day, it has become richer, less numerous, less class-conscious and less revolutionary . . .   (*Ibid.*: 101–2)

This depends on one's definition: if wealth is measured without inflationary adjustments and without regard to the discrepancy between the income and wealth of the upper 1 per cent of society compared to the bottom 50 per cent of the same society, then Magee is right; otherwise, he is wrong. Moreover, many of the contributing factors for the increased wealth of the working class are due to Marxist-like reforms, such as labour unions, that promoted workplace safety rules and ensured minimum wages and health care provision by the owners of the means of production.

> Communism could be brought about only by the workers themselves, the masses: in fact in no country to this day, not even in Chile, has the Communist party managed to get the support of the majority in a free election . . .   (*Ibid.*: 101–2)

Ever since Marx, and especially since the various International Communist Congresses, it was clear that the intellectual class should be integrated into this revolutionary process. Leadership will have to be cultivated and the workers must be educated. Incidentally, public education is available in most capitalist states as a measure of goodwill and self-interest: to ensure qualified workers in an ever-changing technoscientific environment.

> Ownership of the Capitalist means of production was bound to become concentrated in fewer and fewer hands: in fact, with the development of the joint-stock company, ownership has become so widely dispersed that control has passed into the hands of a new class of professional managers . . .
> (*Ibid.*: 101–2)

One can only scan any statistical data concerning the concentration of wealth, however defined, to see that less than one half of 1 per cent of any society owns more than two thirds of the society's wealth. Check the list of the twenty wealthiest individuals or the *Fortune Magazine*'s one hundred international corporations and the culture will repeat itself. It is true that more workers have a stake in their companies or in other companies where their pension funds are invested; but pensions that enable individuals to retire at a specific age and expect their former employers to provide for them are increasingly becoming a thing of the past. One could suggest that the diffusion of stock ownership is a capitalist ploy to expand the reaches of the owners of production, a pretence of sharing ownership with workers while maintaining full control of all decision-making and offering preferred stock categories for dividend and bonuses purposes. The managerial class has wrested power from workers' representatives, such that the real large stockholders become the stake-owners who participate in decision-making. From my own perspective, this slow transformation of capitalism by its own doing and with regard to some of the ideals of Marx illustrates that Marx's own critique and predictions are contextually bound by a view of capitalism that itself becomes a moving and changing target. As Magee says:

> and the emergence of this class is itself a refutation of the Marxist prediction that all other classes would inevitably disappear and be polarized into two, an ever shrinking Capitalist class which owned and controlled but did not work, and an ever expanding proletariat which worked but did not own or control. *(Ibid.*: 101–2)

The professional class is a complex of many subdivisions, especially when professionals are nothing but workers who own nothing, and who still live from paycheque to paycheque, knowing full well that they can be fired and replaced at will. Besides, this is still a description of the permutation of Marxist observations, not a refutation of the division into classes wherein one small class owns and controls the majority of the means of production.

But instead of trying to redefine the terms and seem defensive in light of the critique levelled by Magee, let me suggest a paradox. Either Marx is right and Magee misses the points he makes, or Marx was wrong in his predictions and then they are falsified, and then he has provided a scientific theory. Either way Marx's theory looks much better than Magee claims it to be.

Scientific methodology as social practice

Roberta Corvi, another sympathetic critic, follows the standard approach to Popper's scholarship and begins with Popper's methodological insights as applied predominantly to the natural sciences. Through following this path, her critical summary and evaluation help shed light on my concern with Popper's view as permeating all areas of research, natural and social. In her words: "Not even falsification, then, leads to absolutely indubitable results, although the degree of uncertainty is quite different from the impossibility in principle (not merely de facto or by chance) of verification" (Corvi 1997: 23). Setting the stage for appreciating Popper's insistence on searching for truth through a path of trials and errors, not avoiding errors but documenting them rigorously so as to learn from them and know for sure what is not the case, she agrees with Popper that the "central problem in the philosophy of knowledge" should be structured in three segments:

> (1) the problem of demarcation between science and non-science (primitive magic, myth, metaphysics); (2) the problem concerning the rationality of scientific procedure; (3) the problem of the acceptance of theories for scientific and practical ends . . . [this structure of the problem] led him not only to delineate a new concept of science, but also to make more precise the notion of rationality underlying the whole Western tradition in both philosophy and science.   (*Ibid*.: 26)

With this triad, Corvi joins the group of critics who observe in Popper's texts an overarching concern with knowledge, rationality and science as means to broad social and political ends, and not as ends in themselves. Popper never confines himself to scientific methodology and its variants, nor to a critique of his predecessors and interlocutors alone. He always keeps a keen eye on the political conditions within which science can be practised, the social structures where freedom of opinion is welcomed or discouraged, and the moral standards that guide human interaction.

Corvi reminds us of the difference between falsification, when a theory or principle of knowledge claim has been falsified, and falsifiability, when a theory has the potential for being falsified, even if it never in fact is falsified (*Ibid*.: 28). She continues to explain that "the probability of a theory is thus inversely proportional to its empirical content", so that testing theories through falsifying instances is most successful in the cases where the theory is on logical grounds considered less probable. This is a more technical way of encouraging, in Popper's terms, a critical spirit in testing theories and their attendant statements or conclusions, so that the more severe they are, the better (*Ibid*.: 41). She continues and uses Popper's own words:

> Popper is concerned to draw a clear distinction between the idea of approximation to the truth (that is, verisimilitude) and the idea of probability with which it has often been confused

> . . . verisimilitude . . . combines truth and content while prob-
> ability combines truth with lack of content. (*Ibid.*: 43)

This is important in explaining the kind of "objectivity" Popper
has in mind. For him it is not the result of "neutral and impartial
observation" but rather a social "institution" of sorts that encourages "inter-subjective" rational criticism (*Ibid.*: 44). We can notice
here that the Popperian scientific method which is commonly
taken as a first step towards secondary steps in application elsewhere (economics, politics, etc.) is presented as itself being a product of or dependent on social institutions: rationality is not a
value-neutral, objective, disembodied concept, but a product of
a lively, personal engagement of critical individuals who eventually
reach some temporal agreement about this or that piece of information or knowledge claim. This way of thinking leads Corvi quite
easily to the appreciation that in the social sciences, just as in the
natural sciences, we may conclude about what cannot be the case,
about the errors of our conjectures, about what we should exclude
from consideration because of failures (*Ibid.*: 48–9). Just as physi-
cists learn from their errors in the laboratory and the observation
of natural phenomena, so can politicians learn from their errors
when implementing social and economic policies.

"Criticism", which is the inter-subjective activity of rational
individuals who are encouraged to interact with impunity, "is
the instrument with which we try to draw closer to the truth and
even lay hold of it, although it remains impossible to rest upon a
foundation of certainty" (*Ibid.*: 138). Once again, this statement is
true in natural and social matters, true when applied to scientific
methodology and political platforms. It is on this ground, too, that
Popper's critique and rejection of utopian thinking as totalitarian
comes into play: the presumed certainty with which a utopian
vision is implemented flies in the face of the kind of rational criticism Popper demands in all affairs. How can political leaders be
so sure? What guarantees of certainty do they have? How dare
they surpass the timid level of certainty (understood as measures
of probability) that scientists enjoy? Is it because they refuse to
learn from their own mistakes and change their views over time? It
is in this sense that they become closed-minded totalitarians and
fascists!

Corvi suggests that although Popper agrees that meaning cannot be found in history as such, we can bring meaning to it, and confer what we decide the meaning should be, especially when we do so in light of an ethical approach that in itself need not seem futile (*Ibid.*: 76). This is also Popper's critique of the great thinkers who claimed to find meaning in history as if it were a natural phenomenon one "discovers", rather than appreciating the extent to which we, as observers and thinkers, confer meaning on what we observe in history. We approach a historical period from our own perspective, and we impute to it whatever values are closest to our own. Popper, like any other twentieth-century thinker, could not have missed the opposite interpretations offered by Hegel and Marx regarding the historical record. It was their own meaning that they saw, for Hegel it was a historical progress, moving the world Spirit from one epoch to another, while for Marx it was class struggle and the crises embedded in economic conditions of society that drove us closer and closer to capitalism and its own demise. Where Hegel saw an improvement towards higher levels of understanding and human fulfilment, Marx saw the deprivation of the human spirit that would lead inevitably to a revolutionary moment when human fulfilment will take over the sanguine progress dictated by bourgeois complicity with oppression of the majority and the enjoyment of the few.

Along these lines of argumentation, we can see how Corvi points out that Popper switches the demarcation between realism and idealism into one between determinism and indeterminism; both, obviously, are metaphysical claims about the world as a whole, but the second set, she claims, makes more sense for Popper's general approach (*Ibid.*: 109). Note that idealism and realism could be identified as the labels appropriate for Hegel and Marx, respectively, but that determinism and indeterminism are more commonly identified as the labels appropriate for logical positivism and perhaps quantum mechanics, respectively. The metaphysical framework associated with any of these four terms, however applied in the natural or the social or the human sciences, is at the heart of Popper's approach and critique. It is this recognition that sets him apart from his Vienna Circle colleagues and many of his detractors, since for all of them the very notion that metaphysics plays a part in their thinking and in the work of scientists seems anathema, a dangerous admission, an intellectual hazard one must avoid at all costs.

Corvi is sympathetic to Popper's concerns, and as such bridges the metaphysical elements that ground his thinking about science with his thinking about society. She notes that, for Popper, "physical determinism is rejected on the grounds that it does away with the ideas of creativity and human freedom" (*Ibid*.: 117). Physical determinism has been replaced in the natural sciences by the twentieth century as an untenable metaphysical commitment worthy of Newton and his theories. One may adopt the nuclear physical view or Heisenberg's Uncertainty Principle; one might agree that at the sub-atomic level energy follows its own rules of indeterminism, where space and time are variables that cannot be both arrested for exact measurement, or be left wondering about the origins of the universe and the peculiarities of the Big Bang theory and Black Holes. However, it remains clear that any sort of "physical determinism" is a marginal view applicable to fairly small and circumscribed and artificially constructed contexts. But how does this transform or translate into the social sciences, into historical developments, and human interactions?

Corvi answers for Popper that any kind of determinism is detrimental for human freedom and creativity, detrimental to anything we hope for in our own time and for future generations. If everything is predetermined, then what use is there for us to think, to act, or to invent? If all of our thinking has been prefigured, and all of our actions are nothing but reactions, and all of our inventions are nothing but reincarnations of previously known ideas and objects, then why even bother to live any more? On metaphysical and even religious grounds, Popper sides squarely with the notion of free will over predetermination and fate; for him, to be human is to have the freedom to choose and act, however foolishly, but to do so creatively and individually.

When one moves from the metaphysical level and the individual level to the social and political level, Corvi reminds us of Popper's insightful comments:

> Popper also warns us to mistrust those who want to rule by love rather than reason: to love others means to want to make them happy, and there is a danger that happiness – even that

> of others – will be defined on the basis of one's own scale
> of values, which almost inevitably clashes with other scales of
> values and leads to hatred and intolerance.　　(*Ibid.*: 154)

Popper has no problem taking love away from the equation that guides one's rule of a society, as long as it is replaced by reason. It is reason, and not love, that he wants to see at the heart of the scientific enterprise, and it is reason, and not love, that he wants to see in the affairs of the state. Love sounds like an appealing component of one's leadership, loving one's people in order to bring about happiness, but whose happiness is being considered? How does one measure one's happiness against another? What standards of measurement shall be used? It is with these questions that one's love as an emotive substitute for rational thinking is challenged and not as an inappropriate component or element in one's political rule as such. Of course, Popper wants some compassion, too, but this is different from love as such.

One should love one's people, but not rule accordingly alone; one should listen to one's people, but not rule accordingly alone; one should use one's charisma, but not rule accordingly alone. Only when all of these elements or components of a leader are critically evaluated and rationally harnessed can we hope to avoid the hazards of an emotive rule, the kind seen often during World War II in Europe. What personal price was paid in the name of love, the love of one's *volk* or the love of one's nation? How many innocent lives have been lost in the name of love? Even Hitler couched his venom against the Jews and gypsies, the Catholic clerics and the communists, in terms of his love for the Aryan people and their happiness without them. According to Popper, it was Hitler's irrationalism that did him in at the end, and it was that irrationalism that should have alerted everyone from the beginning that he was dangerous and an unfit leader. But love carried the day, and with it the doomsday of Europe.

Corvi's main criticism of Popper is that, for some, the "unity" of Popper's thought is reduced to a "monotony" since everything is based on his Logic (*Ibid.*: 160). This means that not everything is reducible to logical configuration or that not everything can be evaluated in terms of its logical structure and stability. In some cases logic is not as useful as in others. In some cases, such as falling in love, logic is overshadowed or non-existent. Obviously, the leftist intellectuals have understood Popper's ideas and methods, whether connected to his critical rationalism or logical positivism, to be conservative rather than gradualist, protecting the existing power relations and social order set by capitalism, rather than a champion of change in the name of justice. She shows how easy it is to turn him into a hero or villain, depending how one applies his method and principles (*Ibid.*: 170–71). This goes along with the critical evaluation already mentioned in the previous section regarding the procedural or methodological approach Popper, like Kant before him, favours. Yes, Popper can be interpreted as supporting ideas and policies that would be reprehensible; yes, he would rather move slowly to reform a bad situation than overthrow it completely; and yes, his gradualist approach has the disadvantage of being slow in changing the existing order. All of these Popper takes to be the virtues of his approach, since they allow him to watch for errors and correct his choices along the way before it's too late. But these so-called virtues, too, can be considered a cowardly way of dealing with grave situations that demand swift changes.

Critical rationalism

The definitive summary and assessment of Popper's critical rationalism is provided in Joseph Agassi and Ian Jarvie's edited volume *Rationality: The Critical View* (1987). In it, they have brought together various views and applications of Popper's notion of rationalism seen methodologically or functionally as a process of criticism. They suggest that from Popper's 1935 work on the rational foundation of science, a foundation whose criteria of demarcation (as falsification) turned around the standard justification of the Vienna Circle inductivists, to his 1945 work on the critical rationalist approach of "rationality as the [Socratic] dialectic of interrogation", there is a thread that in effect ties these two works. Elsewhere Agassi notes in this context the nuanced shift undertaken by Popper on the question of the foundation of rationality. For the positivists, all moral, metaphysical and theological statements were meaningless; for Popper they were beyond the rational realm, since they weren't empirical or logical in the strict sense. But since they weren't meaningless, they could still be studied, and when he developed his position between 1935 and 1945, he realized that "indeed rationality has an irrational basis, but that it is most rational to minimize that basis. The minimum, he claims, is the Socratic assumption that we can learn from our mistakes" (Agassi 1971: 33). In his critical assessment of Popper's view of rationality, Agassi would like to modify Popper's view: "The view advocated by Popper: rationality is critical debate; the modification suggested here is: rationality is not any critical debate, but only that which is oriented towards a specific goal as well as might be reasonably expected" (*Ibid.*: 34). Put differently, Popper's preoccupation with the history and practice of science shifts the debates from the ontological and metaphysical levels to the methodological, operational levels, and as such they lend themselves to applications in all areas of inquiry. This means that political philosophers, political scientists and politicians are all in a position to examine their agendas and concerns, their approaches and the public response to these approaches, in a manner that differs from the previous two standard views of Karl Marx and Max Weber, to pick two major examples.

While the Marxian approach considers the material conditions of any situation as the determining factors with which to assess current circumstances and future developments, the Weberian approach is more ideological in the sense of figuring out the prevailing metaphysical convictions of a society and the roots of its belief system as guides for institutional structure and individual behaviour. Against this backdrop, the Popperian approach tries to shy away from metaphysical examination on the one hand, acknowledging how important a role metaphysical commitments play in any venture, including scientific inquiry, and a reductionist move on the other, whether it be psychological or another. The heart of the matter is, as Agassi suggests, one's attitude towards the relationship between institutions or societies and individualism, especially in the sense that Popper's contribution has been all along his conjectural and bold positioning of the ideas of thinkers, such as Socrates and Marx, and of intellectual enterprises, such as science and politics. We'll return to this point in Chapter 3, but at this point it remains an important characteristic of those concerned with critical rationalism. The most important element emphasized by Agassi is Popper's insistence that the individual actor, as a critical rationalist, takes responsibility for a decision or choice made by her or him. Moreover, although the choice to be rational or to behave rationally remains, on some level, a leap of faith of sorts and as such is an irrational act, it's a choice one makes in order to interact with others in a society. A society does not think or act, as holistic or collectivist thinkers maintain, since it's composed of individuals whose thoughts and actions make a difference in what happens to the society as a whole (*Ibid.*: Chapter 9). Hopefully, one's actions, rational and critical as they are of one's own previous actions and those of others, take into account the rational behaviour of others in choosing what to do and how to do it.

In Agassi's scheme, one can note how holism and collectivism, the views that society is a whole which is more than its parts and that society affects individual aims, respectively lead to institutional analysis where society constraints individual behaviour. Likewise, one can note how individualism and the rationality principle, the views that only individuals have aims and that individuals behave in a way adequate to their set aims, lead to institutional reform where society changes according to people's actions (*Ibid.*: 121). I shall refrain from discussing the details of the views surveyed by Agassi on behalf of a Popperian assessment of the social sciences; instead, we should recall that psychologism, the view that all behaviour is reducible to the psychological dispositions of individuals, has been jettisoned from this analysis. This, incidentally, is similar to Popper's approach regarding the development and growth of scientific knowledge. For him, it is a *logical*, and not a capricious or irrational, decision-making process. This is the main point of contention between him and Thomas Kuhn (1970), for example, whose own description of the historical record of the scientific enterprise ends up assigning the honorific title of revolutionary paradigm shifts to instances that have no internal logic or a reason for having happened in this, rather than that, manner. For Popper, by contrast, the idea that there is a method and that the method is based on rationality, and that rationality is nothing more than a critical approach anyone can adopt, is itself an idea about human reason, individual rational thought, and personal responsibility. The last point is significant because it's not an accident that happens and then one cannot reconstruct what has taken place; rather, when adopting the critical approach, one must admit to having made mistakes and then corrected them, to have tried to refute or falsify a theory or an idea or a statement, and then figured out how to revise the theory, idea, or statement.

The process of what Popper calls "conjectures and refutations" is in tune with our humanity, and as such appeals to our rational faculties and not to our emotional baggage. It's also in this sense, then, that Popper has less to say about human nature as such and more about this or that decision that this or that individual has made at this or that point in time. The contextualization of the Popperian approach is at once quite forgiving (because it is individual) and fairly demanding (because the individual is not off the hook in the name of society or any other group affiliation). This brings us full circle to ethics (*Ibid.*, Ernest Gellner, Chapter 8), and especially to the view of ethics not as a theoretical construct or a principled foundation (in Kant's sense or any other), but in the Greek sense of Socrates and even Aristotle. For it was in their teachings that individuals learned to think for themselves, find virtue in their actions, and defend or attack the consequences of their actions, whether intended or not. Rationality is not an absolute tactic or methodology, nor is it a Weberian *Ideal Type* whose reality is not to be found in this or that instance. Instead, it is a practised activity one formulates and perfects, one eschews or refuses to use. It is something that allows us to interact and ask each other questions, critically interrogate ourselves and others so as to figure out not only *what* we are doing but also *why* we are doing it.

This, too, brings us back to Popper's insistence that individuals are the primary variables in any investigations and not the group or society to which they belong. Popper's reluctance to appreciate utopian thinking and relegate it to the category of totalitarian thinking comes into play here, for the collectivist and holist are willing to sacrifice individual rights and pleasures, needs and wants, in the name of the larger good or promise. This price is too high to pay for Popper and his disciples, perhaps because of what they experienced during World War II, perhaps because any policy or platform that does not put the individual at its centre is suspect and potentially dangerous. Ideologically, then, Popper holds to some notion of individualism such that it brings about the greatest potential for improvement and progress of the group. If it were not so removed from religious consideration, almost dogmatically so, one could see here the biblical creation story, where Adam is created by God and put at the centre of the universe to rule his domain with divine wisdom. But this still leaves open the question of the political institutions and legal structures within which individuals interact with each other.

We recall that Popper's view of democracy as a political system that allows governments to be overthrown with relative ease and without violence is itself operational only in the negative sense. That is, this view only presents the boundary conditions of change and reform, but has nothing to say about the actual policies and goals to be accomplished by such a political system. If under democracy we can change governments easily but all governments end up self-serving and corrupt, we might as well adopt a benevolent monarchy where kings and queens ensure the health care of their subjects, for example. So, there must be substantial components and goals associated with democracy. Perhaps it is Popper's own peculiar application from science to politics that obscures his vision: it might be sufficient in science to ensure refutability and falsification in principle to keep scientists honest and open to criticism (rather than dogmatic and authoritarian, powerful and abusive) so as to advance the growth of knowledge where there should be no goals or limits except the smooth continuation of the process itself. But can we say the same of our political and social and moral life? Can we remain so open-ended in our processes that we have no idea where we'd like to end up? This line of criticism is outlined by Agassi (1971: 35) so as to remind ourselves that the very agendas we set up should themselves be democratically proposed and debated, where goals and the means to achieve them should be critically examined in a democratic fashion. What this means at the end of the day, and how this indeed mirrors Popper's concern with individualism, is the fact that the meekest voice might overturn a scientific theory or a political structure, that anyone is entitled to have her or his say, and that whatever is said should be taken *prima facie* to be of some rational and critical import.

CHAPTER 2
Capitalism as economic equality and freedom

Four main themes inform this chapter. First is the particular context of the turn of the twentieth century in Vienna that included what was termed the "methodological war" or "struggle" (*methodenstreit*), which would reaffirm some of the issues already discussed in Chapter 1 concerning the underlying methodological issues in the study of all the sciences. The second theme is the confusion that marks any attempt to demarcate between politics and economics, especially as it relates to the concepts of equality and freedom (with the classical tension that alleges that the more the one, the less the other). The third is the specific concerns voiced by Popper in relation to economic theory, both in terms of its methodology as a unique area of research among the social sciences; and fourth, some of the contemporary uses and misuses of Popper's own views on economic theory and its scientific status.

Historical context

Anyone consulting contemporary textbooks in economics will notice the extent to which many economic assumptions rely heavily on psychological principles and theories, regardless of their validity in their own field of research. To some extent, the so-called Austrian School of Economics of the beginning of the twentieth century exemplifies this reliance as against the German Historical School. Although some historians, like Hacohen (2000: 462ff.) suggest that the contention was between Gustav Schmoller of the German Historical School and Carl Menger of the Austrian School of Economics, I suggest looking historically at an earlier period.

The crux of the dispute between these two schools is the different emphasis either placed on material historical developments that affect the economy and the economic behaviour of individuals: the Historical School followed some Marxian notion of the social forces of society that evolve in certain patterns and could be noticed in the market place, while the Austrian School followed the classical English and Scottish thinkers (Hume, Smith and Ricardo for example) and emphasized the centrality of individual behaviour patterns on the marketplace. Carl Menger was among the first three economists (with Jevons and Walras) to articulate the principle of marginal utility which is itself drawn from the psychological principle of diminishing return of personal satisfaction (the more chocolate or ice cream you eat, the less exciting the experience, the less money you are willing to pay for the last ounce as compared with the first).

Already at this stage, one can notice how Popper fits into this mould. He himself, as Hacohen reminds us, was interested in both psychology and Marxism in his youth, and therefore was familiar with these issues and personally concerned with finding solutions to the problems they posed. Historians and biographers are probably more qualified to find exact lines of connection or causal relations between this or that text and this or that idea that is found in Popper's work. I would like to point out the natural progression of the thought of the era in which Popper writes and to explain the degree to which the ideas of economists were aligned with or paralleled his own ideas. But here another cautionary comment is in order. Economists of the turn of the twentieth century saw themselves as political economists, as social theorists, as public intellectuals. They were government officials at some point, academics at another, and authors at a third point. The interwoven personal experiences of so many of the European intellectuals differ radically from what we understand today as economists, primarily academic or think-tank number crunchers who quantify solutions to economic problems with the latest mathematical tools at hand. It's within context, then, that Popper is no different from Menger or Hayek in participating in and contributing to economic thought.

Back to Menger. What Menger understood from the start is that the fight over methodology is crucial for overturning one economic framework and replacing it with another. Whether Joseph Schumpeter was right or wrong to suggest that economics should be thought of as applied psychology is beside the point (Schumpeter 1977: 1057). But he managed to recast classical economic theory from the eighteenth century into its neo-classical mode of the late nineteenth century and early twentieth century. Perhaps it may be useful to rehearse some of the basic economic principles advocated by Menger and accepted into the mainstream of thinking by the time Hayek and Popper come along. To begin with, Menger offers the following with regard to the free exchange of goods among individuals, by contrast to any Marxian analysis of the historical stages of economic forces:

> (a) one economizing individual must have command of goods which have smaller value to him than other quantities of goods at the disposal of another economizing individual who evaluates the goods in reverse fashion, (b) the two economizing individuals must have recognized this relationship, and (c) they must have the power actually to perform the exchange of goods.   (Menger [1871] 1950: 180)

This sounds familiar to anyone who has read Adam Smith's landmark treatise on the market place ([1776] 1937), where the "invisible hand" guarantees the free exchange of goods and services among individuals. Although Menger's account is more informed in terms of the psychological theories that developed during the late nineteenth century, and although he was less "hedonistic" in his approach (Smith emphasized self-interest rather than altruistic behaviour), he is still concerned with setting up a system of exchange that depends on people's (rational) behaviour. Incidentally, it is exactly this rationalist twist that turns economic analysis into a so-called science capable of quantification. In Menger's words:

> But what has been said by no means excludes the possibility that stupid men may, as a result of their defective knowledge, sometimes estimate the importance of various satisfactions in a manner contrary to their real importance. Even individuals whose economic activity is conducted rationally, and who

therefore certainly endeavor to recognize the true importance of satisfaction in order to gain an accurate foundation for their economic activity, are subject to error. Error is inseparable from all human knowledge. (*Ibid.*: 148)

Although the emphasis is on subjective decision-making, and although there is an assumption about economic behaviour being rational, Menger is one of the first to incorporate error into his model. Humans not only make mistakes when they behave irrationally; they might make mistakes when behaving seemingly rationally. This means, in the final analysis, that all knowledge (both of the participants and of their observers) is bound to be incomplete and prone to errors. If we extend this way of thinking into Popper's own work, we see right away what methodological innovation Popper offered: instead of avoiding errors (since they are unavoidable in principle and in practice), focus on them and eliminate them in your hypothesis construction so that you can know for sure what is not the case (rather than pretending, with the inductivists, that your accumulated observations lead to absolute and certain knowledge). (See Sassower 1985: Ch. 5.)

We must never forget that Menger was a European thinker of the old school, namely, a thinker whose intellectual reach transcended his preoccupation with economic theory as a science alone. Let me illustrate this with a couple of quotations that show how at one point he insists on separating economics as a science from all political and moral considerations, and on the other hand, he's still aware that tradition and custom influence human behaviour (so that science alone, or logical analysis by itself, couldn't dissect or explain or predict it). In his words:

Among other things, our science has the task of exploring why and under what conditions the services of land and capital display economic character, attain value, and can be exchanged for quantities of other economic goods (prices). But it seems to me that the question of the legal and moral character of these facts is beyond the sphere of our science.

(Menger 1871: 173)

... custom and practice contributed in no small degree to converting the commodities that were most saleable at a given time into commodities that came to be accepted, not merely by many, but by all economizing individuals in exchange for their own commodities. (*Ibid.*: 261)

Menger is aware that custom and habit, as Hume used to call them, affect human behaviour and are themselves not reducible to the rules of logic or the components and methods used by science. Of course, for Hume there are other issues at hand, especially as they relate to institutions or societies as a whole as well as to individuals, in some sense of psychologism (a view that is reductionist in some senses and prone to rational reconstruction in other senses). Yet, he would like to keep economic theory as scientific as possible by not engaging in political and legal and moral questions. This tension was relinquished by the Hegelian–Marxian dialectics when suggesting that every variable played a role in the whole of society, in analysing and predicting its next shifts and moves, its next developments. But Menger and the Austrians, after seeing what this path led to in terms of the historical justification for revolutionary activities, decided to revert back to a line of epistemological and intellectual isolation, where their research and investigations could be limited to the scientific enterprise, however broadly defined. Of course, finding Popper along the way, Menger's disciples were relieved that his ideas and writings could be hitched to their own, especially since his starting point was physics and inquiries into other natural sciences.

As Hacohen emphasizes, the *methodenstreit* was about methodology in the social sciences, including economics, and therefore questions about holism or the reality of universal laws were raised in contrast to the emergent economic "laws" and models as propounded by the Austrians as a way to circumscribe their reach and applicability. Popper's *Poverty of Historicism* is seen as a direct response to some of these questions (Hacohen 2000: 464). The Austrian genealogy moved from Menger to von Mises and Hayek, both of whom accepted the empirical and individualistic basis of Menger's methodological innovation in proposing marginal utility as the lynchpin according to which the market place works. Their own contributions were always in light of their disdain for and fear of the historical, Marxist approach of their German counterparts, because they believed that it led to national planning and totalitarianism. It's here that Hacohen correctly suggests the Austrian appreciation of the connection between methodological debates and politics:

> Later generations of Austrian economists argued that intimate connections existed between the historical school's methodology and politics . . . As Mises and Hayek were engaged in an intellectual crusade against Marxism and economic planning, they argued that left- and right-wing socialism both led to totalitarian dictatorship. (*Ibid.*: 465)

So, what is at stake at this juncture is less the contentious atmosphere that informed the economic theorists of the late nineteenth century, but their realization that there is a chain of relations that pervades the intellectual world. If you start from individualistic decision-making processes, you'll end up constructing an economic model that will have different results and different potential for predictability than if you begin with historical laws of economic behaviour that discount imperfection in the rational behaviour of individuals.

Let me add a simple observation that is inspired by the ideas of Paul Rosenstein-Rodan (in conversation and not referenced textually). Planning sounds bad for the Austrians and Popperians because it's about coercion and the muddled thinking of bureaucrats or dictators whose own wills trump the wills of all other individuals. But what kind of planning are we talking about? The old-fashioned view was concerned with the control of natural resources and their allocation for production. This necessarily entailed planning for and control of labour needs in manufacturing and distribution. Consumer needs and wants were last on the list, since what was more urgent was an industrial infrastructure or military build-up. This planning model is collectivist in the worst sense of the term, and seems to have no redeeming qualities, because it fosters a certain national paranoia against any mistakes one might make in predicting future needs and resources and the means by which to balance them optimally; in short it is totalitarian.

Two issues must be considered in relation to this kind of a model of planning. First, over-emphasizing infrastructure or war effort if undertaken for short-term periods (under two years) may be important, necessary and valuable. We should recall that during World War II, for example, there was no hesitation about or concern with government planning in the United States and Europe. "Big Science" projects were promoted for national security and war effort not only in the Manhattan Project but also all the way to munitions and food supplies. America needed to defeat fascism; America needed to mobilize its collective power in the name of freedom. So, planning as such is not necessarily inappropriate, as we can see. Moreover, more often than not, planning is useful, even efficient from an economic standpoint. Secondly, it is not planning as such that is the problem, but particular kinds of planning that drew the ire of the Austrian School and Popper. Their complaints were about planning that was autocratic and wouldn't deviate from its course, the kind that would not change course when mistakes were discovered, when alternatives were offered. Moreover, as Rosenstein-Rodan used to say, the exchange of information and the concerted effort to share information among participants in the market place make it essential for government agencies to contribute their authority and propose soft and mutable planning: should we expand the city in this direction? What is the population flow into the region and how should banks lower their interest rates?

To some extent, the Japanese learned how to do this in their rebuilding of the economy after World War II when they disseminated commercially valuable public information. More recently, we can see examples of such behaviour when the Federal Reserve Board in the United States plays the role of "planning", collecting information from different regions, monitoring growth patterns and investment cycles in the economy and dictating a national interest rate (the Prime Rate) that affects all financial activities in every sector of the economy. Is this still considered planning in the traditional sense, or is this a new variant unknown a century before and therefore despised on principle, without regard to its beneficial elements and its stabilizing force on the economy? This is not to say that economists such as Rosenstein-Rodan are pro-planning and are socialists at heart. Instead, this is to remind us that sometimes planning is beneficial, sometimes detrimental. If you limit your analysis to economic matters, equilibria conditions are preferred to chaotic cycles. If you think of economic analysis in political, social and moral terms, then the argument becomes more interesting with more counter-examples to any categorical statement anyone makes. Recalling the post-World War II era, there was no other way to rebuild both western Europe and Japan without "planning"; the Marshall Plan is still considered one of the glory moments and great achievements of the war, so much so that it has been evoked repeatedly in international affairs as a justification for foreign intervention when disasters afflict nations. What concerned Rosenstein-Rodan is the tendency to throw away the baby with the bathwater, as he used to say. Planning, for him, was a matter of degree and not of kind. I'm using him in this context for two reasons: he, too, was a Viennese refugee that found himself in London and eventually as the head of MIT's economics department, and also because he was one of the Committee of Nine who was responsible for the economic restructuring of Europe after the war (he was "in charge" of Italy).

Back to the Austrian School and Popper. I would agree with Hacohen's assessment that at times it seems that drawing the battle lines between the Austrians and the Germans was more important rhetorically, and perhaps nationally, than the actual issues they argued about. For example, he cites some points of agreement and disagreement Popper should have had with Menger's ideas, but the fact that Popper didn't read Menger's books and the fact that he was friends with von Mises and Hayek who admired Menger made him soft-paddle his critique or not even voice it. Hacohen writes:

> Popper expressed agreement with Menger on methodological individualism, the causal, formal, and exact nature of scientific theory, and the methodological unity of science . . . He limited his open dissent to Menger's distinction between exact and empirical types, but, in fact, they disagreed on crucial methodological issues. Not only was Menger an "essentialist," but his argument that exact theories were nonempirical and non-testable also made them metaphysical at best, spellbinding at worst. Providing precise and definite (short-range)

forecasts for testing was crucial for Popper. This was just what Menger denied that exact theory could do.

(Hacohen 2000: 468–9)

Hacohen's astute observation of the nuanced discussion among the theorists of the early twentieth century highlights some of the issues to which I'll return in the next section, namely, the confusion between and juxtaposition of social, economic, political and moral concerns. In order to appreciate what was going on at the time, two quick remarks might suffice. On the one hand, there was a belief in or aspiration for the unity of the sciences (at least methodologically, by positivists and others alike), so that any field of research and interest was thought to be parallel with any other, and one set of ideas pertinent in one could be therefore easily applied in another. On the other hand, since the Hegelian–Marxist path to knowledge and happiness was charted along historical, evolutionary lines, and the metaphysical conviction regarding the inevitability of certain processes and outcomes, it stands to reason that economic thought was subsumed as part of this intellectual framework. If one agrees with these two comments, then it stands to reason that lines of disputations would revolve around the socialist or communist agenda as it was proposed between the two world wars in the European context.

Back to Ludwig von Mises, the "father" of the Austrian School. In his book on epistemology of 1933, he recapitulates the main issues distinguishing, in his mind, economic theory from other areas of study, such as art, primarily because of its predictive powers:

> Economics is a theory capable of making assertions about future economic action, about the economic conditions of tomorrow and the day after tomorrow. The concept of theory, in contradistinction to the concept of history, is . . . understood as involving a regularity valid for the future as well as for the past.   (von Mises 1933: xx)

Continuing with the distinction between the historical approach that brings "understanding" into its framework because it employs moral concepts and principles and the theoretical one that is based on logic and the scientific method, von Mises says:

> The purpose of this book is to establish the logical legitimacy of the science that has for its object the universally valid laws of human action, i.e., laws that claim validity without respect to the place, time, race, nationality, or class of the actor. The aims of these investigations is not to draw up the program of a new science, but to show what the science with which we are already acquainted has in view. (*Ibid.*: xxii)

What the Austrians were seeking, and that is why the flirtation with the Vienna School and with Popper makes so much sense, was a way to legitimate that which they were already doing: they needed the vocabulary and methods of the natural sciences and the lines of demarcation against the non- or pseudo-sciences so that their own "investigations" could be validated and implemented into policy. The affinity to Popper, in particular, is most pronounced in the following statement, where von Mises wants to eschew the historical method of induction:

> What is under attack here is the doctrine that would have us believe, on the one hand, that historical data can be approached without any theory of action, and, on the other hand, that an empirical theory of action can be derived by induction from the data of history. (*Ibid.*)

Since on the political agenda was the fight against the new variants of socialist thinking that were engulfing central Europe before and after World War I, these epistemological musings about what we know and how we get to know it have a definite and relevant impact on one's model construction and eventual application of the theory. It therefore makes sense to recall an earlier text by von Mises that directly tackles socialism.

In his *Socialism* of 1922, von Mises defines socialism as: "a policy which aims at constructing a society in which the means of production are socialized", and capitalism as:

> the realization of what we should call economic democracy . . . a system in which the workers, as producers, and not as consumers themselves, would decide what was to be produced and how . . . the power to dispose of the means of production, which belongs to entrepreneurs and capitalists, can only be

acquired by the means of the consumers' ballot, held daily in the market-place.   (von Mises 1981: 10–11)

These definitions in themselves are not disputed in Mises' work and the work of his disciples; instead, it is the role of logic and science that is brought into light once again. According to von Mises, Marxism was an attempt to bring a socialist framework within logical and scientific lines of argument, establishing it not as an ideology or a utopian vision, but as an inevitable reality logic could prove. According to von Mises, Marxism used "three lines of procedure":

> First, it denied that Logic is universally valid for all mankind and for all ages. Thought, it stated, was determined by the class of thinkers; was in fact an "ideological superstructure" of their class interests. The type of reasoning which had refuted the socialist idea was "revealed" as "bourgeois" reasoning, an apology for capitalism.   (*Ibid.*: 6)

Surely there is a difference between universal logic and a line of reasoning. It's true that Hegel's books on logic were supposed to explain reason and rationality, logic, as dialectical and evolutionary, moving from one stage of simplification and abstraction to more general ones. It is also true that Marx's critique of classical economics was based on the interpretive elements one brings to bear on model construction in so far as one uses or interprets one set of assumptions differently from another, based on one's situation and circumstances, one's culture. This insight has been swallowed wholesale by philosophers of science who have studied the history of science and realized how shifts in understanding can recast one set of observations in light of different assumptions or paradigms. I would venture to claim here that Popper's own writings are much more like Marx's in this sense: namely, he has taken the liberty to reinterpret the data, empirical or textual, so as to provide novel propositions and ideas, whether in his writings on political philosophy or on science proper.

Von Mises continues:

> Secondly, it laid it down that the dialectical development led of necessity to Socialism; that the aim and end of all history was

61

> the socialization of the means of production by the expropria-
> tion of the expropriators – the negation of negation.   (*Ibid.*)

It is true that the Hegelian–Marxist dialectical movement of history pushed into certain directions rather than others, and it is also
true that there was inevitability or necessity in this movement in so
far as it was the next logical step or stage for the development to
be. But it is unclear exactly what socialism would mean once the
means of production were not privately owned. The idea that the
public would control everything is appealing and problematic
because government agencies as representatives of the public's will
could be benign, benevolent, or autocratic. Rousseau was aware
of this in his *Social Contract* just as Socrates and Plato were aware
of this in the *Republic*. To vilify socialist ideals in the name of the
Soviet Union, as already mentioned in Chapter 1, is to overlook
the "aim" (as von Mises calls it) of socialism as an economic reality meant to improve the standard of living of all citizens (as the
Scandinavian countries have attempted in the late twentieth century). Perhaps part of the problem is the minimalist definition von
Mises uses, simply focusing on the ownership of the means of production, which is just one of the many features and concerns and
goals that come under that definition.

Von Mises continues:

> Finally, it was ruled that no one should be allowed to put
> forward, as the Utopians have done, any definite proposals
> for the construction of the Socialist Promised Land. Since the
> coming of Socialism was inevitable, Science would best renounce
> all attempts to determine its future.   (*Ibid.*)

It is fascinating to note here that although von Mises claims that
Marxism utilized logic and science to fight old versions of socialism, he also claims that logic and science were shunned by the late
nineteenth-century Marxists. Perhaps the only way to understand
this seeming contradiction of von Mises' indictment is by looking
at his 1950s Preface in which he divides the contemporary world
into "two hostile camps . . . Communists and anti-Communists"
(*Ibid.*: 1). Moreover, the so-called progressive socialists/communists
are lumped together with "Italian Fascists and German Nazis".

Once the ledger is set this way, there are obviously enemies that ought to be fought and demolished, shown to be wrong-headed from the outset with poor methodology, without logic, and with prejudicial irrationality that leads to totalitarianism.

Indeed, there is a slippery slope one is bound to encounter if the dichotomy between socialism and capitalism is set in these particular terms and if socialism is given even an iota of scientific respectability. If socialism is based on logic, and if logical structure is a necessary (although not sufficient) condition for scientific status, then the predictions coming out of this framework can command credibility beyond the ideals of utopian thinkers who dream and hope for a better world. But if socialism is denied any scientific credibility from the outset, then nothing that is said on its behalf would make sense unless one is a believer, a follower, a blind disciple. It is exactly here where the Austrian School needed to find philosophers of science, like Popper, as allies, and it is on this level that Popper's own concerns matched those of his intellectual predecessors and contemporaries. Although one might be talking about quantum mechanics or about marginal utility, one still needed to be adept at using the best tools of the trade (mathematics and logic, induction and deduction, laboratory measuring instruments, and precise critical analysis). In doing so, one ended up enmeshed in the methodological web of the scientific community, however narrowly or broadly it was defined (both the web and the community). It was under these intellectual and practical conditions that political alliances were formed as well.

Political economy as economic theory and political agenda

All the Austrian critics of Marxism had one thing in common: they appreciated the overall framework of Marxism as incorporating everything from metaphysics to physics, economics and politics, morality and religion. No area of research or of life that affected human behaviour was allowed to remain untouched. But it is exactly here that something awkward was happening to them all: they added the emphasis of science and its pristine credibility and objectivity, its value-neutrality and openness, its logical structure and rational transparency, its explanatory and predictive powers, and its self-policing integrity. Once everything is measured against the ideals of the scientific community, the standards of credibility rise as well. Put differently, by the dawn of the twentieth century, to confer on anything scientific status means to confer on it certain authority and legitimacy that cannot be gained elsewhere (no matter how much one pays). Marxist theory was attacked on its scientific status by the Austrian School as well as by Popper, but along the way the critics committed their own mistakes; they fell into the abyss of ideological disputations where critical rational discourse recedes to the background, where rhetorical force and passionate convictions carry the day (are you with us or are you our enemy?). Agassi suggests that when Popper quarrels with the demarcation of Marx's and Freud's theories as being scientific he has this kind of prestige and status in mind. But when he offers his own demarcation he seems to forget to be self-critical and ask the same question of his own criteria: does refutability confer honour? Obviously, this would be a different kind of honour, yet it would be a demand for status just as dogmatic or strict as the one suggested by the others.

But before I continue, I would like to clarify three points. First, one can be a socialist in economic terms but advocate a democracy (as can be seen in Israel) or a dictatorship (as can be seen in Cuba or the former Yugoslavia); likewise, one can advocate a democratic political structure but ensure socialist planning for a major segment of the economy (in a manner close to the welfare programmes found in the Scandinavian states). One can find a military dictatorship that protects a capitalist economy (as was the case in Chile for four decades). So political structures may differ as to the kind of legal protection they provide in the most efficient or traditional manner to the market place. No market place can survive on its own; it needs the political and legal grounding to ensure its functioning (for more on this see Karl Polanyi 1944). For example, if one advocates competition, one must ensure that it can flourish and be maintained; this can happen only if those who fall behind are not completely jettisoned from the market place or are barred from entering it; this can happen only if there are certain legal protections, such as bankruptcy laws, anti-trust laws that prohibit unfair competition or the collusion among large corporations who can control the market place in terms of limiting supplies of goods or services, or refusing to pay for labour or raw materials or whatever is being asked. Secondly, the issues that seem to characterize socialism versus capitalism in terms of property ownership cannot be simplified to the extent that the former advocates public and the latter private ownership of property. For example, many European and American capitalist democracies have enormous tracts of land that are publicly owned and maintained for the safety and pleasure of the population as such (in the United States 20 per cent of the land mass is publicly owned and controlled through the Department of the Interior). We have, even under neo-classical and neo-conservative models, room for public goods, such as roads and bridges, airports and shipyards, military forces and fire departments. There is a deep sense that no matter how rich or poor one is, these kinds of services would be equally available to all. So, there is no real or actual manifestation of all of these *Ideal Types* in Weber's sense that use labels, such as socialism and capitalism. And thirdly, there is a historical context within which theories and models are developed and pursued. Usually they come about as a critical response to theories and models that fail or that seem unfair, unjust, abusive and painful. On this, Marx and Popper agree, although Popper would like us to think that to think historically leads inevitably to a kind of historicism he rejects; obviously, Popper's own historically informed thinking does not commit him to a narrowly focused and reductionist path that others tend to take (some of this was discussed in the previous chapter and will be dealt with in the next chapter as well).

Oddly enough, in his most popular and provocative book, *The Road to Serfdom* (1944), Hayek explains quite clearly the different notions of liberty embedded in the literature and sometimes misconstrued (because these notions are detached from their historical context). In this, he helps clarify the kind of confusion that plagued the Austrian School in its *methodenstreit*. The subtitle of his book is: "A classical warning against the dangers to freedom inherent in social planning". It is in this text, among many others, that we see clearly the conflation of economics and politics, sociology and morality, and the ways in which the arguments about the loss of freedom cannot be squarely and narrowly put on a specific version of socialism known in the late nineteenth century, or its attempt of implementation in Austria or the Soviet Union. As he says:

I use throughout the term "liberal" in the original, nineteenth century sense in which it is still current in Britain. In current American usage [1944] it often means very nearly the opposite of this. It has been part of the camouflage of leftist movements in this country, helped by the muddleheadedness of many who really believe in liberty, that "liberal" has come to mean the advocacy of almost every kind of government control. . . . A conservative movement, by its very nature, is bound to be a defender of established privilege and to lean on the power of government for the protection of privilege. The essence of the liberal position, however, is the denial of all privilege, if privilege is understood in its proper and original meaning of the state granting the protecting rights to some which are not available on equal terms to others.   (Hayek 1944: ix–x)

This passage is quoted at length not only because it is one of the few places where the distinction between the nineteenth-century meaning of liberty in its British context is distinguished from its American counterpart of a later century, but also because of the rhetoric used. So, on the one hand we see "privilege" as an important category for what liberalism is not, and on the other hand we see "government control" as the crucial apparatus through which particular ideological commitments get executed. The protection of privilege is the purview of monarchies and aristocracies; and government control is the purview of monarchies, aristocracies, totalitarian regimes and dictatorships. It should be noted here that the antecedent epistemic privilege (having a preferred standpoint from which to judge the optimal balance between resources and needs, between production and distribution, for example) turns quite often to a political and social (and personal) privilege (having a preferred position that should not be challenged by anyone else outside the small group of commissars, for example). Where is democracy? And what do we mean by it? Is it enough, as the Austrians suggest and eventually the Chicago School of Economics continues to suggest into the present century, that one "votes" with one's wallet? We might even agree that economic freedom is necessary for political freedom; but is not the reverse true as well? How is it possible to have such freedoms? What legal structures ought to be in place, and how should they be formulated, and by whom?

Although the French and American Revolutions of the eighteenth century are presented as models for democratizing the western hemisphere, they too had problems associated with their execution and with their eventual functioning. Robert Dahl is only one of the most noted political thinkers in America who repeatedly asks us to evaluate how democratic our constitution is. For him, the American constitutional structure is a republican compromise between the aristocratic and democratic tendencies that informed the founding fathers. Not only does he question the role of the Senate and the Electoral College (as hindrances to direct and equal representation), but he also suggests that the very notion of a government has been brought into question: even if representational, in what sense? (Dahl 2001)

Fritz Machlup's essay on Hayek illustrates, from a more technical and limited perspective, four main features of Hayek's thought on economics. First, that his main contributions transcend the marginalist revolution of his predecessors in Vienna (quantifying tastes and preferences and appreciating marginal returns on satisfaction, investment, consumption, production, labour and capital) to the area of business cycles (including trade, labour and capital cycles). Secondly, since Hayek was engaged in developing and revising economic models that dealt with cycles in the market place, he was consumed by methodological issues that concerned all scientists (natural and social), namely, the nature of reality, causal relations among factors, and the appropriate representation of said reality (or its *Ideal Typical* conditions). Thirdly, the appreciation of economic cycles is one that leads to explanatory and predictive models; this being the case, though, it necessarily pushes economic theory from academic institutions to government agencies and policy makers at all levels. A cycle can be enhanced or retarded, heralded among the public as a miracle of the willing or a disaster of greed and stupidity. With a pen-stroke, policy makers can shut borders or raise tariffs of goods and services, increase or decrease the interest rates charged by central banks or simply print more or less money (when gold is no longer the standard bearer of value and, to some, credibility). Fourthly, as he notes in relation to Maynard Keynes and his general theory of business and economic cycles (the interconnectedness between investment, saving and consumption, or between production, distribution and consumption), this was an important theoretical foundation for the New Deal policies after the Great Depression in the United States in the late twenties and early thirties. Government intervention was useful in getting the economic machinery back into action. Hayek, by contrast, advocated a "wait and see" policy that would have been disastrous. There are, then, implications to one's theoretical formulations, and the policies enacted in the name of a theory bear consequences on people's lives (Machlup 1977: 26).

What Machlup acknowledges right here is the interwoven relationship between theory and practice, between economics and politics, and between one's ideological commitments and one's policies (as an individual and as a nation). None of this, of course, is fundamentally different from what Karl Marx, for one, said. The difference, though, is more strategic than epistemological. The Austrian School, just like Marx, wanted to understand how the market place works and what impediments there were to its successful alleviation of poverty and suffering. Marx was more radical in his belief that they could be eliminated once and for all (after the revolution), whereas the classical and neo-classical economists thought it would be a long process that could be successful in raising the overall standard of living (the reformist, gradualist procedure Popper endorsed). Under the naive view of Adam Smith, the free exchange of goods and services by individuals within an open and equally accessible market place was attainable. But already Smith alerted his readers both to the problems associated with over-specialization and so-called job fragmentation and to the potential for abuse, where the rich would gang up on the poor and would have unfair advantage when exchanging goods and services. Smith's own warning and prescription were forgotten, but his original vision was retained (despite being unrealistic). In relation to the price of labour in the marketplace, Smith says:

> The workmen desire to get as much, the masters to give as little as possible . . . It is not, however, difficult to foresee which of the two parties must, upon ordinary occasions, have the

advantage in the dispute, and force the other into a compliance with their terms. The masters, being fewer in number, can combine much more easily; and the law, besides, authorises [*sic*], or at least does not prohibit their combinations, while it prohibits that of the workmen.　　　(Smith [1776] 1937: 66)

The realization that there was an unfair market advantage to one group over another, so that in point of fact no individual faces the market place as an individual, capable to engage in free exchange with every other, illustrates Smith's foresight and his uncanny ability to anticipate Marx's work. Moreover, Smith was keenly aware of the legal mechanisms in place to favour one group over another. It's in this sense that Smith's model has never been fully appreciated for its inherent problems, and always been misused as if it were a descriptive and prescriptive model exclusive of any political, social and legal contexts.

As Marx read the classical economists, he, too, was worried about abuses, and therefore suggested class alliances to gain sufficient bargaining power by the "workmen" in Smith's terms so as to minimize, if not eliminate, exploitation and alienation by the "masters" in Smith's terms. The Austrian School and Popper agreed with all of the above, but suggested a different idealized version of the capitalist market place, or perhaps different strategies to ensure its viability, one that both assumes and ensures individual freedom as its very core. Must individual freedom be at the expense of equality and vice versa? All political economists have struggled with this question. It seems that the more freedom individuals are granted, the more likely it will be that some will prosper at the expense of others. Some call it meritocracy, the view that merit alone should dictate human behaviour and social conventions, so that those most deserving will end up ruling, financially and politically, those who are less deserving. This view is touted as being superior to the view that those who inherit more money and power deserve to keep it despite their incompetence.

If we agree that economic theory is supposed to be scientific but also a theory of human action, with all the psychological underpinnings that such a theory inherently requires, we can immediately detect potential problems. Likewise, if we agree that economic theory is supposed to be scientific (and not historical) but also to lend itself to predictions and policy recommendations, we can likewise immediately detect potential problems. These tentative agreements, I suggest, can be found in the debates surrounding the Austrian School with the Historical Schools of Germany and England at the time. With this in mind, von Mises reminds us that:

> One combats economics because one knows no other way to protect an untenable political program against unfavorable criticism that employs the findings of science . . . it is not out of place to point out that abstract problems of logic and methodology have a close bearing on the life of every individual and on the fate of our entire culture.
>
> (von Mises 1933: xxvi)

Two issues come to light here: the first relates to how an economic theory becomes the battleground for policy matters – is it scientific enough? Does it adhere to the rules of logic? Is it merely a pretence of logic but in fact has no logic to it at all? The second is that so-called academic disputes about the logical status of economic theory are indeed important to the welfare of a culture. In other words, worrying about the epistemological foundations of economic theory is no idle task, but rather a necessary starting point for anyone concerned with human behaviour within a culture.

Popper's own concerns with economic theory

Perhaps we should recall in brief some of Popper's most explicit statements and ideas concerning economics or economic theory or political economy. I shall provide some highlights of his own treatment of economics, economic theory, and economic methodology in a chronological order. In doing so, I'll avoid repeating quoted passages that appear either earlier in this chapter or in the previous chapter. For example, in his early work, *The Logic of Scientific Discovery* ([1935] 1959), Popper says the following:

> Science can be viewed from various standpoints, not only from that of epistemology; for example, we can look at it as a

biological or as a sociological phenomenon. As such, it can be described as a tool, or an instrument, comparable perhaps to some of our industrial machinery. Science may be regarded as a means of production – as the last word in "roundabout production". Even from this point of view science is no more closely connected with "our experience" than other instruments or means of production.   (Popper [1935] 1959: 100)

Although Popper does not directly address economics in his major treatise on the methodology of the natural sciences, his language is pregnant with images and terms borrowed from economic theory. His use of the "means of production" already foreshadows his interest in and concern with the Marxist theory of economics as a theory focused on the ownership of the means of production. The fact that "science" is compared here with instruments and with a productive tool for industry and culture already hints at later discussion of the partly conventionalist nature of scientific theories, namely, the fact that they are not "real" in any strong sense of the term, but culturally informed (even though not arbitrary!).

In his *The Open Society and Its Enemies*, as we already saw, Popper reminds us that unlike "the magical or tribal or collectivist society" which he calls the closed society, the open society is one "in which individuals are confronted with personal decisions" (Popper [1943] 1966: I, 173). It is from this standpoint that economic analysis of human behaviour comes into play, for there is a great emphasis on personal decision in light of what he calls "rational reflection". If one's behaviour is irrational, it namely follows magical or tribal suggestions or pressures, then there is no reflection associated with it: one does what one is expected to do! But if one has the freedom to choose, then one must figure out, especially when one makes a mistake and gets hurt, what criteria were used in choosing; this process of reflection, according to Popper, is rational in so far as it is critical, and it's critical in so far as it has been reflective.

Obviously when Popper tackles Hegel and Marx, he is even more concerned with economic theory and its scientific status by the twentieth century. Instead of reviewing all the details of Popper's critique of Marx's economic theory, and instead of following the standard interpretation of Popper's critique of Marx as if he despised his theories and found no merit in them, let me give an example of the ways in which Popper agrees with Marx, and even gives him credit for anticipating some theoretical developments in the analysis of market capitalism. The particular example used here is of the trade cycles and the fact that perfect market conditions to stabilize supply and demand may not hold. To begin with, he says:

> We should have to show that the buying and selling on the market produces, as one of the unwanted social repercussions of our actions, the trade cycle. The Marxist theory of the trade cycle has precisely this aim in view . . . the mere fact that Marx treated this problem extensively is greatly to his credit. This much at least of his prophecy has come true, for the time being; the tendency towards an increase in productivity continues: the trade cycle also continues, and its continuation is likely to lead to interventionist counter-measures and therefore to a further restriction of the free market system; a development which conforms to Marx's prophecy that the trade cycle would be one of the factors that must bring about the downfall of the unrestrained system of capitalism. And to this, we must add that other piece of successful prophecy, namely, that the association of the workers would be another important factor in this process. (*Ibid.*: II, 196)

In this passage, Popper credits Marx with providing a coherent and accurate analysis of the trade cycle, its causes and its eventual outcomes or effects in so far as they disrupt the so-called equilibrium of the markets. Whether it is increased productivity or increased cheap imports makes little difference in figuring out that some intervention is bound to happen so as to rein in or combat disequilibrium in the markets, in the way of tariffs or changes in the cost of capital or of transportation, for example. Likewise, Popper is sensitive, just as Adam Smith was, to the fact that because of market cycles there are incentives to collaborate and form more powerful bargaining units to ensure stable wages, for example, or stable employment. Of course, Popper terms Marx's prediction "prophecy", but that is no different from the general attitude of disdain espoused by the Austrian School towards the

Historical Schools. Surely the term prediction would have lent some scientific credibility to Marx's analysis, but Popper would not grant him that much, since he is still concerned with the those in Europe who call themselves socialists and Marxists, but whose political agenda is not as sophisticated as Marx's own in relation to the study of capitalism. They have reduced everything to abuse and exploitation, without realizing that capitalism as an economic system may break down on its own, if it does not have the legal and political protection to ensure its own survival and evolution.

I should hasten to say that I'm not trying to turn Popper into Marx or suggest that there is no critical dissension; rather, I would like to emphasize how much Popper is openly and explicitly indebted to Marx by his own admission in understanding of economic theory, perhaps even more than his indebtedness to the Austrian School which was more of a "party line", so to speak, regarding what is the appropriate method to use when studying human affairs. In one of the most careful and friendly discussions of capitalism as a label or term used at the time, Popper suggests in a footnote the following:

> The term "capitalism" is much too vague to be used as a name of a definite historical period. The term "capitalism" was originally used in a disparaging sense, and it has retained this sense ("system favouring big profits made by people who do not work") in popular usage. But at the same time it has also been used in a neutral scientific sense, but with many different meanings. In so far as, according to Marx, all accumulations of means of production may be termed "capital," we may even say that "capitalism" is in a certain sense synonymous with "industrialism." We could in this sense quite correctly describe a communist society, in which the state owns all capital, as "state-capitalism." For these reasons, I suggest using the name *"unrestrained capitalism"* for that period which Marx analysed and christened "capitalism," and the name *"interventionism"* for our own period. The name "interventionism" could indeed cover the three main types of social engineering in our time: the collectivist interventionism of Russia; the democratic interventionism of Sweden and the

"Smaller Democracies" and the New Deal in America; and even the fascist methods of regimented economy. What Marx called "capitalism" – i.e. unrestrained capitalism – has completely "withered away" in the twentieth century.

([1943] 1966: II, 335)

On some level, this is probably the most informative passage about the use of categories relating to economics we have seen so far. Earlier I have tried to distinguish between capitalism as an economic system and the different political and legal frameworks within which it can flourish or be restrained. And here Popper provides the classical sense of unrestrained capitalism as an *Ideal Type* of sorts, an abstract and perhaps unachievable economic system, that may require some sort of intervention to protect itself from either falling apart (because of cyclical crises) or becoming abusive and exploitive to the extent that it would undermine if not destroy any sense of individual freedom. Popper's acknowledged sensitivity to this point could have been highlighted more by his disciples, but they took on different paths to elucidate and apply his ideas on scientific methodology.

It's fascinating to observe Popper's continued insistence on separating economics from all other social sciences in other contexts, as he does in his *The Poverty of Historicism* (1957). Time and again, he lauds and praises economic theory for using mathematical methods, attempting to check theoretical claims against facts, and being concerned with solving social and political problems (Popper 1957: 56–7). Since in this book Popper advocates piecemeal engineering, and since he also wishes to elucidate the methods most appropriate for the social sciences in alliance with the natural sciences, he suggests looking at social experiments and learning from our errors:

A grocer who opens a new shop is conducting a social experiment; and even a man who joins a queue before a theatre gains experimental technological knowledge which he may utilize by having his seat reserved next time, which again is a social experiment. And we should not forget that only practical experiments have taught buyers and sellers on the markets the lesson that prices are liable to be lowered by every increase of supply, and raised by every increase of demand.   (*Ibid.*: 86)

Popper explains that problems of measurement as applied to the social sciences and the ability to use quantitative methods in economic theory in particular have been partially handled by the use of statistical analysis (*Ibid.*: 142). Here, too, Popper wants to push economic thinking from a theoretical and qualitative analysis (that is, interpretive and historical, and therefore not scientific) to a more quantitative level that can measure actual situations and predict specific outcomes (and therefore become scientific in this sense). In short, if economics is to avoid the fate of the other social sciences as unscientific in Popper's sense, then it must be more mathematically based and have the kind of methodological rigour that would qualify it to be a science. His reliance on the work of the Austrian School and the neo-classical economists gives credence to the claim that regardless of the assumptions used in economics and regardless of the starting conditions of any situation, if humans are somewhat rational their behaviour can be mathematically analysed, their preferences can be quantified, and with a bit of statistics one can predict the outcome of any set of economic variables.

In his *Conjectures and Refutations* of 1963, a book dedicated to Hayek, Popper spars once again with Marx's ideas, but gives him credit for turning around the Hegelian dialectic:

I think it is a fair interpretation of the ideas of Marx and Engels to say that one of their chief interests in emphasizing materialism was to dismiss any theory which, referring to the rational or spiritual nature of man, maintains that sociology has to be based on an idealist or spiritualist basis, or on the analysis of reason. In opposition to this they stressed the fact that the material side of human nature – and more particularly the need for food and other material goods – is of basic importance for sociology.

This view was undoubtedly sound; and I hold Marx's contributions on this point to be of real significance and lasting influence. Everyone learned from Marx that the development even of ideas cannot be fully understood if the history of ideas is treated (although such a treatment may often have its great merits) without mentioning the conditions of their origin and the situation of their originators, among which conditions the economic aspect is highly significant. Nevertheless I personally think that Marx's economism – his emphasis on the economic background as the ultimate basis of any sort of development – is mistaken and in fact untenable. I think that social experience clearly shows that under certain circumstances the influence of ideas (perhaps supported by propaganda) can outweigh and supersede economic forces. Besides, granted that it is impossible fully to understand mental developments without understanding their economic background, it is at least as impossible to understand economic developments without understanding the development of, for instance, scientific or religious ideas. 　　　　　(Popper 1963: 332)

We should mention at this juncture that the main intellectual antidote to Marx was Max Weber, who emphasized how much ideas and beliefs, including religious ones, had an influence on one's behaviour as an individual and on the moral ethos of a culture as a whole (e.g. *The Protestant Ethic and the Spirit of Capitalism* originally of 1904–5; incidentally, the behaviour of guilds and the kind of commerce prevalent during the Renaissance, for example, could be tied to Catholic ideals just as much as was done by Weber). So, it is not that Marx was not a post-Hegelian pioneer of adding a materialist basis for historical analysis, worrying about the empirical conditions under which the culture lived and from which one should start constructing explanatory and predictive models, but that he was too much so. This might be considered a parallel complaint to the one levelled by Popper against the Vienna Circle: they, too, insisted on verification and confirmation of theories by empirical data and shunned anything outside the material realm of observable "facts", but in doing so they overlooked the metaphysical elements of any theory construction and one's ability to conjecture hypotheses that may or may not be confirmed or falsified by empirical data (whether in principle or in practice). (See especially Part I of Popper's *Logic* [1935] 1959.)

In his intellectual autobiography, Popper explicitly says that, although he was invited to the London School of Economics, and although he was concerned with methodological issues as they related to the social sciences:

> Yet the social sciences never had for me the same attraction as the theoretical natural sciences. In fact, the only theoretical social science which appealed to me was economics. But like many before me I was interested to compare the natural and social sciences from the point of view of their methods, which was to some extent a continuation of work I had done in *The Poverty*.   (Popper 1975: 121)

He singles out economics, perhaps as a boundary case of the kind of science that could, under certain circumstances, be considered "natural" as opposed to "social". Since one of Popper's main and lasting contribution to the philosophy of science is his outline of the problem of demarcation (between science and non- or pseudo-science), it stands to reason that he would be attracted to debates that could confirm or falsify his own criteria of demarcation: economic theory fitted the bill. Moreover, Popper's interest in economics went beyond the application of his criteria of demarcation, since he was keenly aware of the policy potential that rested with the putative credibility of economic theory: one can further a political or moral agenda based on what an economic model will predict will be the outcome of certain regulatory policies. I suggest that these issues might be intellectually and theoretically as important as the practical consequences of the particular policies chosen in this or that country. It might also explain the personal affinity and friendship Popper sought and found in the Austrian School and those fighting the rise of European fascism between the two world wars. Perhaps this would be a good point in the discussion to move to some of Popper's students and disciples who extended his ideas into this area of discussion.

Contemporary uses and misuses of Popper's ideas

There are three major paths one could take from Popper's ideas about economic theory and the methodology of economics. I shall briefly review them without going into detail with regard to any of them. The first, and perhaps the most useful and interesting path, was taken by some of Popper's students, research assistants and disciples. In it they undertook to explain and expand the ideas of the master who was fairly unknown outside his own small circle in the United Kingdom. I shall mention only three of them, oddly enough all immigrants and refugees of sorts, who might have found as much personal affinity with Popper as with his ideas. I should probably explain what I mean by this. It seems to me that Popper's obsession with critical rationality is a twofold demand: to be rational first and foremost, and to be critical at all times about everything. The quest for and belief in rationality dates back to the Enlightenment ideals, already mentioned in Chapter 1, but finds new lustre, post nineteenth-century attempts to subvert and reinterpret its principles and classical application. The appeal is for universal communication and general appeal, one that transcends parochial or ethnic differences, one that can provide the groundwork for any future peace and harmony (à la Kant). The refugees I have in mind (including Popper) were surely drawn by this central article of faith. Likewise, the critical attitude and demeanour fitted well with displaced intellectuals who were in better positions than their indigenous counterparts to simultaneously observe everything (theoretical and practical) from the inside and the outside. Who better equipped to stop and question every assumption, every convention, and every conclusion? It stands to reason that no assumption or ideas would be taken for granted or would implicitly be accepted; just like Socrates, the dialectical process of questioning, of trial and error, or conjectures and refutations, is never-ending. Being a foreigner, as Nathaniel Laor (1990) reminds us, is similar to being afflicted with schizophrenia, where multiple languages are invoked and thus create inevitable dissonance that may lead to crises or insights, depending on the circumstances. I would cheerfully report that in the case of the Popperians, many insights came forth.

Pulling together conference papers of 1965 and editing them for publication by 1970, Imre Lakatos and Alan Musgrave (1970) were able to pit Popper's ideas against one of the most popular of American methodologists, Thomas Kuhn (notorious for his obscure term "paradigm" that some claim is defined in more than thirty different ways in his text of 1970). In this collection, Lakatos himself develops one of the most eloquent extensions of Popper's methodology, so as not to have it dismissed as either too naive or abstract. In offering his notion of a "research programme", Lakatos tries to illustrate how hypothetical bundles of theories evolve over time, changing some of their outer extensions because of refutations, but holding on to some "hard core" (Lakatos & Musgrave 1970: 91–196). In this essay, Lakatos is interested in examples from the natural sciences and ignores economics, for example, and other social sciences. His main concern is the growth of scientific knowledge and the ability to appraise a set of theories rather than evaluate theories one by one with strict criteria. But instead of going over the details of his insightful elaboration and revision of the Popperian "core", I would simply like to report here that this is one of the students/disciples who pushed on with the programme, who accepted the basic Popperian tenets and fought the Kuhnian programme as being fundamentally irrationalist (because no explanation can be given to paradigm changes and the new directions they take). In Lakatos's work (1976) we see historical research and scholarship to buttress his outlook, as he does, for example, in his book on mathematics, suggesting there that the method of conjectures and refutations can be easily detected in the historical record of mathematical theory and practice.

Joseph Agassi and Paul Feyerabend were also students/disciples with a much sharper critical approach and dissent regarding the master's basic ideas. Although Feyerabend (1975) does not directly address questions about economic theory and practice, he does suggest an alternative that arises out of the Popperian mould but seems to undermine it. Instead of looking for rationality as the basis of all intellectual knowledge and the growth of the scientific enterprise, Feyerabend argues that the fixation on method alone is misguided. Instead of worrying about the appropriate choice of methodology and its appropriate application, he is more concerned with the fluidity of methods of inquiry and the blurred distinction between scientific knowledge and all other kinds of knowledge. As far as Feyerabend is concerned, the actual outcomes of a theory or model or principle count for more than its construction. Wanting to appear as a rebel, Feyerabend uses the kind of rhetoric that he knows would infuriate Popper, but in order to maintain some intellectual respectability, his text is measured and argued along rational lines, and it also provides extensive historical anecdotes to support each claim and argument. In short, however "anarchistic" he wishes to present his ideas, he remains a Popperian pragmatist who could have drawn alliances with American thinkers, such as Charles Peirce and W. V. O. Quine.

Joseph Agassi is probably the most prolific and underappreciated of the students/disciples of Popper, having written on as many topics as the master has and some more (from physics to politics, technology and art, psychology and sociology, mathematics and economics). Instead of surveying his enormous output, I shall point out three main themes that seem to qualify and redirect the Popperian trajectory. First, Agassi noted that although Popper was concerned with the demarcation problem and with scientific methodology, he never quite took social and economic and political issues straight on (even in his *Open Society*). By contrast, Agassi always poses the questions: why is the problem of demarcation important and for whom? What difference does it make if we approach it from this or that perspective? When answering these questions, Agassi tends to be less dogmatic about the criteria of the master, and is willing to find an epistemological and methodological middle ground that is at once pragmatic (as mentioned in connection with Feyerabend) and applicable to policy makers (see Agassi 1975 and 1981). Secondly, Agassi was one of the first to recognize that the scientific enterprise was not as pristine or abstract or pure as the philosophers of science took it to be. In pushing this line of discussion, he has become a pioneer in the area of the philosophy of technology, and saw the intimate interrelations that exist between science and technology, both on theoretical and practical grounds (Agassi 1985). And thirdly, he was one of the few from amongst the Popperian camp who took on the master and who wanted to engage him on a critical level. His numerous publications eventually drew the ire of Popper, so much so that no intervention could reconcile the rift. It's here where the personal and emotional element of the camp comes into expression.

Perhaps this is a useful transition, from discussing Popper's disciples to figuring out if there ever was or still is a Popperian camp or school, the way we discuss the Vienna Circle and the Austrian School. I guess the principles by which each member was to operate were self-destructive to any cohesive group-like behaviour. Not only was Popper himself reticent to join any group or school of thought (unless it was Socrates and his circle, or Kant and his way of thinking), but he insisted on individualism as a catchword and methodological necessity (as I shall discuss in the next chapter). So, with rabid individualism it is impossible to get group affinity and affiliation, a feeling of mutual admiration and compromise. Moreover, if one is fiercely committed to critical analysis, to refutation and falsification, as honorific means of legitimation, then this would be the first and lasting approach one would receive from any Popperian, old or young. Intellectual camaraderie or mutual assistance are conveyed through bitter and personal attacks that are deemed rational and critical, merely a device to clarify what is being said and ensure that it is properly open to further criticism. And finally, since any supra-human control and intervention are considered totalitarian, fascist, and fundamentally inappropriate from the Popperian perspective, no organization can be formed, no club or centre established. As we shall see shortly, the only one who is currently attempting to rectify this is George Soros (but this, too, is a flawed attempt).

It seems to me that the group of students/disciples of Popper that were with him between the 1950s and the 1970s set in motion the eventual recognition of the importance of his ideas and their usefulness in the discussion of all methodological matters. There were applications of his ideas in art (by Gombrich 1960) and anthropology (by Gellner 1974), for example, but I shall focus here on the ways in which scholars appropriated his ideas in economics. On the one hand you have some, like Lawrence Boland, who have made some insightful contributions to economic methodology but who have remained outside the mainstream of the establishment (that is more concerned with econometrics and investment application), and even my own contribution to the field (Sassower 1985). Unlike Boland the economist, my own concern was philosophical in so far as I tried to illustrate how Popper's problem of demarcation and methodology could be assigned to diverse economic theories, all of which would fail his rigorous tests. For me, the questions were: should economic theory be granted a special status among the social sciences? Should economic theory, given the past two centuries, command respect and power as a scientific enterprise? If yes, why? If not, why not? Moreover, once granted scientific legitimacy, what are the political consequences that follow? Does such legitimacy in and of itself entail any preferences for specific policies, or does it mean, instead, that policy recommendations will be shielded from close scrutiny and criticism because they are deemed to be "scientific" in some particular sense (and therefore it makes sense to enlist philosophers of science for the job). Finally, I thought that the questions were in fact poorly stated, since they assumed a lot about the scientific enterprise (its credibility, objectivity, value-neutrality, etc.), rather than use the historical examples of economic theory to pose questions about the scientific enterprise itself. Here, too, Popper could be an inspiration (as we shall also see in the next chapter) when he unabashedly introduces metaphysics into the fray, and accepts the problems associated with the notion of objectivity (individuals versus a process of inquiry).

On the other hand, there were numerous working economists who did exactly what I thought should not be done: use Popper's views and ideas as the means by which to bolster the reputation of economics. Just as Kuhn's notion of a paradigm was widely used as a cry for scientific respectability by any field of research – if we have a paradigm then we are a science; if we are in a pre-paradigm stage, then we are not – so was the case with Popper's criteria of demarcation. The problem with Popper and his disciples, of course, is that their own positivist stance was a bit more nuanced than Popper's Viennese colleagues and their disciples. Disputes over inductivism and rationalism, theory selection and appraisal, putative truth and the approximation of truth (all in lower case) sounded much less foundational and absolute than one would expect from science.

It is in this light that one can observe the awkward attempts by Daniel Hausman and Mark Blaug, for example, to engage the Popperian apparatus (Hausman 1984). These attempts still run along the same lines of argumentation from the nineteenth century and add little to the literature. Perhaps their most lasting contribution is to provide in the late twentieth century a counterbalance to the narrowing of the field of economics into the exercise of mathematical tools and models with the computational power of high-speed computers. I say this with utmost respect and hope, for any field that refuses to study its own history and the methodological debates that brought it into its current position is a field bound to failure and stagnation. But the short-lived resurgence in the interest of methodological questions related to economic modelling have lasted less than a decade, so that new scholarship is limited to the application of mathematical instruments for the sake of governmental economic forecasting (that have failed to ameliorate cycles) or the investment and profiting of financial institutions.

One beneficiary of the financial basis of and dominance over the capitalist market place as it extended itself to the global economy has been George Soros. A Hungarian refugee, Soros has felt affinity with Popper both on a personal level and also on an intellectual one. For reasons that remain obscure to me, Soros has suggested on numerous occasions that his financial success is attributable to Popper's ideas. Rewriting in 2000 his own 1998 book, Soros makes the following claim:

> Communism sought to abolish the market mechanism and to impose collective control over all economic activities. Market fundamentalism seeks to abolish collective decision-making and to impose the supremacy of market values over all political and social values. Both extremes are wrong. We need to recognize that all human constructs are flawed. Perfection is beyond our reach. We must content ourselves with the second-best: an imperfect society that holds itself open to improvements. Global capitalism is badly in need of improvement.
>
> (Soros 2000: xxiv)

To claim that any human construct is in principle imperfect is neither new nor noteworthy. To claim that human constructs are in need of improvement is also trite. But what has made Soros interesting is his ability to transform what we consider fairly common intellectual ideas and implement a financial strategy that made him a billionaire. How did he accomplish this?

Soros explains the notion of self-fulfilling prophecies in Popper by borrowing the notion of reflexivity from the sociologists of science, suggesting that it adds an element of uncertainty, and one that affects the reaction of people to their situation (*Ibid.*: 4). Adding the dimension of so-called radical fallibility (*Ibid.*: 27ff.), Soros gloatingly suggests that these two assumptions about human constructs and their inherent imperfection allowed him to manipulate currency fluctuations and bet against the British pound and make over one billion dollars in profits. Betting against the trend, or proposing a financial strategy different from the accepted norms of the time, entails a great deal of risk, but also potential for great profits. Financial strategists perform this procedure daily, when they buy stocks of a company and, not knowing if they will appreciate or lose in value, they buy options against them that would mature in a way that allows them to make a profit either way. Financial instruments have become sophisticated enough to gauge the global markets so that investors, like Soros, with billions of dollars in capital, can either spot a trend and follow it, or intervene in a trend and change it by manipulating the current values of stocks, bonds, or currencies as they buy or sell in such large quantities so as to have an impact on said values. In this sense, then, Soros and his colleagues behave much less like capitalists who approach the market place as individuals whose own participation cannot and does not influence the market place itself; rather they are like Soviet bureaucrats who dictate with their enormous influence and pull how the market will behave, or like governments who operate within a capitalist framework and "interfere" in the market place when dictating the flow of money and the rate of interest their central banks charge. If anything is "open" in this strategy, then it is open to a very small group of the super-rich who can dictate market trends; it is definitely not open in the Popperian sense that values individuals, their rationality, and the social institutions that protect them from the tyranny of their leaders.

Although Soros wants to portray himself as a follower of Popper, a Hungarian refugee who happened to become a billionaire, and although he recommends some controls over the potential abuses of market raiders, he is much more like Plato's philosopher-king whose power and wealth give him licence to dictate the global economy as we know it (for example, how much market control, in what areas, and to what extent), but who was not elected to that post by his fellow-citizens. If he indeed believed in reforms, in the kind of piecemeal social engineering advocated by Popper, he would stop all large investment groups from dominating the market place; he would refuse to participate in the financial manipulations that earned him billions (and that were lost by someone else, and worse, that adversely affected the entire global economy), and he would disallow the accumulation of wealth in the hands of less than one half of 1 per cent of the population. Pointing out his philanthropic activities will never make up for the billions of dollars that were lost on the other side of the financial equations, the one from which he personally benefited. Soros's gains, we should remember, came from somewhere: someone lost billions when he made them. Even if the losses were incurred by banks rather than individuals, these banks will have to make up for the losses by increasing interest rates, for example, or charging additional fees to all of their customers or inducing the treasury to raise taxes (if it comes to the central bank). In short, Soros's wealth has been gained at the expense of the multitude of people he claims to care for.

But we should not move to the next chapter with this sorry episode in mind. The market raiders of this world come and go and might be forgotten if it were not for their philanthropy, setting monuments to gain immortality. They do remind us, though, of the importance of establishing and maintaining open societies on all levels. Perhaps Popper's greatest contribution to this ethos was partially due to his nominal knowledge of economics, for the economy is only one of the many variables that control human behaviour and the interactions among individuals within a society. The material conditions are relevant, even essential, in appreciating the conditions under which openness can be achieved but there are other variables and factors that bring about and sustain openness; it is a mind-set, a tradition, and social institutions that help ensure openness and even help to redefine what it means over time. What might have been acceptable and even desirable human freedom in ancient Greek society would be challenged today. This is not to historicize the notion of freedom or open society, but to remember that the problems associated with freedom and openness, as Popper would have phrased it, are real problems that require solutions. These solutions themselves should be contested and revised, so that quibbling over definitions and terminology will not suffice. People's lives are at stake when we theorize, when we philosophize, when we claim to be public intellectuals.

CHAPTER 3

Methodology as applied to individualism

Three main concerns inform this chapter: first, a survey of the so-called Positivist Debate of the 1960s in sociology and the issues it raised primarily in Germany in relation to Popper's methodology; secondly, a comparison of one version of feminist situated-knowledge approach with Popper's own position as a reference point to methodological individualism; and thirdly, a discussion of Popper's recommendations in relation to generalizing about individual behaviour as a framework and prescription for individual autonomy, creativity and responsibility.

Individualism as method and practice: positivism and sociology

There is a sense in which some controversies never die, like some diseases, but merely mutate over time, and erupt here and there. The Positivist Dispute in German sociology (based on a conference in 1961 in Tubingen) is an example. It is an extension of the *Methodenstreit* discussed in the previous chapter. It reintroduced methodological concerns in light of some theoretical developments in the social sciences in general and in sociology in particular. In what follows I shall be less concerned with sociology and its claims for autonomous status in relation to other disciples (as not reducible to psychology or any other science), and more concerned with what, in the Introduction to the volume that summarizes the controversy, David Frisby calls "Ghost in the Machine" positivism. Quoting von Wright's version of August Comte's view, Frisby says that one can discern three basic tenets in positivism:

1. "*Methodological monism,* or the idea of the unity of scientific method amidst the diversity of subject matter of scientific investigation."
2. "The exact natural sciences, in particular mathematical physics, set a methodological ideal for all other sciences."
3. Causal scientific explanation which consists in "the subsumption of individual cases under hypothetically assumed general laws of nature."   (Adorno 1969: xii)

Name calling is undignified, but it seems that it is still practised more often than not, as we see during this controversy, and especially when someone like Popper appears on the scene. Here is our proto-positivist, all seem to say, as if positivism is a clearly defined concept and as if they have never read his own disclaimers to the contrary. There is nothing *positive* or honorific in being labelled a positivist, because as both sides agree it is not about being scientific but scientistic (in Hayek's and Popper's sense of being narrow-minded and limited in one's interest to science alone) (*Ibid.*: xiii–xiv). To claim that all of knowledge is nothing more than scientific knowledge or that no knowledge outside of scientific knowledge has any significance is the main thrust of scientism, and all disputants reject it. Moreover, even those who reject the conflation of positivism and scientism may appreciate the view that some hold of positivism not as the bastion of empiricism or realism, but rather the catchword for an exclusive focus on methodological questions (regardless of the disciple or the subject matter). This view was subject to severe critical comments already in the initial reactions to Kant's emphasis on structure and form and neglect of content. If Popper is the contemporary target, then the question to him is: is your method of conjectures and refutations, or trial and error, applicable anywhere and to anything?

The focus of the controversy was Popper's ideas (his theses, as they were presented at the conference). I shall refrain from listing all twenty-seven of them, but summarize some of the more important ones, according to him, so as to illustrate the extent to which his Frankfurt School interlocutors (especially Adorno, but also Habermas) were in agreement with him on the substance of his theses, and that only their terminology was different, radically different. Popper repeated his mantra that knowledge is accompanied by ignorance and, following Socrates, that the more we learn about our world, the more we realize how little we know and how much more there is to learn. But knowledge itself, according to him, is not the accumulation of data. Investigation starts not from the collection of data but from a problem. As he said, "observation becomes something like a starting-point only if it reveals a problem" (*Ibid.*: 89). Popper continued to formulate his proposed method of inquiry in various ways, and I shall quote only the least technical, more accessible one (titled his Seventh Thesis):

> The tension between knowledge and ignorance leads to problems and to tentative solutions. Yet the tension is never overcome. For it turns out that our knowledge always consists merely of suggestions for tentative solutions. Thus the very idea of knowledge involves, in principle, the possibility that it will turn out to have been a mistake, and therefore a case of ignorance. And the only way of "justifying" our knowledge is itself merely provisional, for it consists in criticism or, more precisely, in an appeal to the fact that so far our attempted solutions appear to withstand even our most severe attempts at criticism.   (*Ibid.*: 90)

From this summary, it is clear that Popper's methodology is just as applicable to the social sciences as it is to the natural sciences. If the thrust is problem solving, and if the attempt is always prone to being mistaken and criticized, revised and replaced with another attempt at a solution, then it really does not matter what the subject matter happens to be. From this perspective, there are no better and no worse observations, only more appropriate or less appropriate empirical data that fit or do not fit a particular solution to a particular problem. As we shall see in the next chapter, this basic tenet of critical rationalism sounds quite similar to some tenets of postmodernism (an idea that might shock if not repel many followers of both postmodernism and critical rationalism).

In his phrasing and formulation, Popper is taking great pains to distinguish his proposals from those advocated by the Vienna Circle and other Logical Positivists, for he wishes to distance himself from what he calls the myth of naturalism. "It is the myth of the inductive character of the methods of the natural sciences, and of the character of the objectivity of the natural sciences." This myth, he continues, has got hold of the social sciences "except perhaps in economics", in so far as the collection of observational reports and empirical data in general have been taken to be essential for grounding and justifying any theoretical framework. Moreover, Popper stressed, there is nothing naturalist about the acceptance of criticism: it is a decision that he recommends, not imposes in any manner. The attitude and outlook that is the quest for naturalistic legitimacy, as one might call it, is based on the myth of naturalism that Popper wishes to dispel. But, as he admits, because his own original work was published within a series controlled by the Logical Positivists, he has been mistaken as a proponent (rather than a critic) of this myth (*Ibid.*: 290). One's reputation is difficult to shake off; the stigma associated with one's work or ideas or person is difficult to change.

Popper's views are themselves open to criticism, for he allows that heroic thinkers, free-thinkers and open-minded individuals, creative and courageous, appear on the stage of history and propose outrageous (seemingly so within the historical context of their appearance) hypotheses that then are critically assessed with attempts at refutation. But is this really how it works? This, too, is a myth of sorts, a historically informed reconstruction. But it is an inspirational portrayal of the growth of knowledge, a way to offer anyone a chance both to forward a conjecture about any problem at hand as well as a chance to publicly criticize any solution already at hand. To a large extent, I would venture to say, this is a political ideal of freedom of speech and of thought that can have enormous psychological effects on individuals. Instead of telling everyone to master the traditional knowledge base and adhere to the ideas accepted by the intellectual and social establishments, there is an encouragement to get "out of the box", to think for oneself and to question everything at hand; in short, this is an old-fashioned (but all too often forgotten) philosophical injunction advocated by Socrates: the unexamined life is not worth living!

Perhaps what makes Popper's ideas the target of the Frankfurt School and others, like Shearmur (1996), who believe in the importance of the social and cultural context as they inform individual thinkers and decision-makers, is his insistence on individualism. But lest he be misunderstood as advocating a Robinson

Crusoe-like solipsism (the view that each person is an island to her or himself and is detached from all influences) the way Ludwig Wittgenstein and Rudolf Carnap did, Popper explains his notion of (scientific) objectivity. For him, this

> is based solely upon a critical tradition which, despite resistance, often makes it possible to criticize a dominant dogma. To put it another way, the objectivity of science is not a matter of the individual scientists but rather the social result of their mutual criticism, of the friendly–hostile division of labour among scientists, of their co-operation and also of their competition. For this reason, it depends, in part, upon a number of social and political circumstances which make this criticism possible. (*Ibid.*: 91)

For Kant, objectivity was achieved through a process of self-reflective intersubjectivity; for the Royal Society of London, objectivity was achieved through multiple independent observation reports; for experimental science, objectivity is achieved through independent repeatability under specified conditions; and for Popper, objectivity is not lodged in the individual researcher, but is rather apparent or comes to light in the overall process of a critical approach that is social in this sense of the term (with co-operation and competition, mutual respect and fierce criticism). Objectivity, then, is to be studied as the sociology of knowledge in terms of the conditions that allow for it to flourish and that sustain its constitutive members as productive scientists (social, natural, or other). In his words:

> Objectivity can only be explained in terms of social ideas such as competition (both of individual scientists and of various schools); tradition (mainly the critical tradition); social institutions (for instance, publication in various competing journals and through various competing publishers; discussion in congresses); the power of the state (its tolerance of free discussion). (*Ibid.*: 96)

Although the usage of the term competition may strike some as belonging to economic theory in general and capitalism in particular,

Popper's usage is more simple and naive, pliable to multiple substitutions and permutations. Indeed, his sense of free competition among individuals and ideas takes on the biological and evolutionary sense of the term, rather than its economic counterpart, namely as a practical mode through which improved ideas progress and evolve over time. Incidentally, this way of thinking also explains Popper's rejection of revolution as an ideal and a means for change. Starting from Darwinian evolutionary theory, Popper suggests that

> organisms evolve by trial and error, and their erroneous trials
> – their erroneous mutations – are eliminated, as a rule, by the
> elimination of the organism which is the "carrier" of the error.
> It is part of my epistemology that, in man, through the evolu-
> tion of a descriptive and argumentative language, all this has
> changed radically. Man has achieved the possibility of being
> *critical of his own tentative trials, of his own theories.* These
> theories are no longer incorporated in his organism, or in his
> genetic system: they may be formulated in books, or in jour-
> nals; and they can be critically discussed, and shown to be
> erroneous, without killing any authors or burning any books:
> without destroying the "carriers" . . . *critical reason is the
> only alternative to violence so far discovered.*   (*Ibid.*: 292)

In a series of theses, Popper has moved the discussion from the concerns of positivism, understood by him as the myth of naturalism, to the concerns of objectivity, and from objectivity as a scientific condition for the quest of truth, he has moved the discussion to the social conditions and frameworks within which individual scientists can most fruitfully function. Moreover, Popper shifts the focus from the individual (so as to avoid psychologism, the reduction of one's behaviour and thought to psychological variables) to the context within which she or he operates, and thereby freely allows for the establishment and maintenance of traditions that foster certain environments that are conducive for the growth of knowledge, for finding solutions to problems, and for refuting erroneous proposals and replacing them with others. As he says (in his twenty-first thesis): "there is no such thing as a purely observational science; there are only sciences in which we theorize (more or less consciously and critically). This of course holds true for the social sciences" (*Ibid.*: 101). And finally, it is within this epistemological framework that seems to emphasize methodological procedures that Popper's social and political ideals come to light. His evolutionary epistemology, incidentally, is quite Marxist, too, for it allows for the incorporation of ideas into individuals and into societies as they move from one period to another, yet it is not so Marxist in that it does not chart periods, especially not in advance, and it assumes that progress comes from having learned from mistakes. Still, it is very much Marxist in that it views intellectual progress as embodying solutions that further material and intellectual survival (for more on this, see Marx Wartofsky 1979).

But lest Popper should be considered too close to the ideas and ideals of the Frankfurt School, he reminds us not to forget the individual scientist and the emotional charge that characterizes her or his work: "Thus the 'objective' or the 'value-free' scientist is hardly an ideal scientist. Without passion we can achieve nothing – certainly not in pure science. The phrase 'the passion for truth' is no mere metaphor" (*Ibid.*: 97). This is reminiscent of Weber's notion of vocation or a calling, namely, the idea that individuals choose to engage in an activity because they are passionate about it, care for it, and are willing to make financial and personal sacrifices for it, regardless of the social rewards gained by it. If Popper does not quite follow Weber, then the difference between them lies in Weber's romantic exaggeration of the passion in a romantic fashion that Popper rejects. Once again, Popper shifts the discussion from the empirical basis of observation reports to the psychological and emotional composition of the individual who commits to fight the tension, as he calls it, between knowledge and ignorance.

This shift to the individual, though, is not a psychologistic shift by any means, just as his historically informed examples are not meant to be historicist. As we shall see in the next section, Popper comes up with a middle ground that he attributes to the *purely objective method* of economics, which he calls "the method of *objective* understanding, or situational logic . . . that can be developed independently of all subjective or psychological ideas" (*Ibid.*: 102). He concedes here the necessity of admitting "understanding" as a social and cognitive category of crucial interest, as Adorno and Habermas have insisted all along. But in his view this category takes on a slightly different meaning:

> The explanations of situational logic described here are rational, theoretical reconstructions. They are oversimplified and overschematized and consequently in general *false*. Nevertheless, they can possess a considerable truth content and they can, in the strictly logical sense, be good approximations to the truth, and better than certain other testable explanations. In this sense, the logical concept of approximation to the truth is indispensable for a social science using the method of situational analysis. Above all, however, situational analysis is rational, empirically criticizable, and capable of improvement.
> (*Ibid.*: 103)

Before we move to examine Popper's notion of situational logic and its more recent reincarnation in other fields of inquiry (how it resonates, for example, with feminist critiques of epistemology and philosophy of science), let me also hint at Popper's concerns with methodological individualism (which will be discussed in the last section of this chapter) and the extent to which Adorno ends up agreeing with most, if not all of Popper's ideas.

Popper concludes his remarks at the 1961 conference with the following suggestion regarding theoretical sociology:

1. Institutions do not act; rather, only individuals act, in or for or through institutions. The general situational logic of these actions will be the theory of the quasi-actions of institutions.
2. We might construct a theory of intended or unintended institutional consequences of purposive action. This could also lead to a theory of the creation and development of institutions. (*Ibid.*: 104)

Popper makes it clear that in the final analysis individuals act and can influence the course of history; they are the ones that ought to be responsible for their own actions, and not revert to some view of the inevitability of an outcome and their own complicity reduced to merely being there, being able to do nothing to stop a certain course of events or merely to hasten it somewhat. It should be noted in this context that the American legal system admits the fiction that a corporation is an individual and then struggles – as it still does – with corporate fraud and guilt, in attempts to find some individuals as the culprits deserving punishment (as opposed to fining corporate violators only). The institutional or corporate shield, then, should not allow individual actors and decision-makers to hide from their own thinking and behaviour, their moral sense and the self-critical dimension of their rationality; in short, responsibility rests all along with individual actors.

Although coming from the Marxist camp, and although steeped in dialectics and the method of immanent critique, Adorno seems to agree with most of Popper's views and ideas, obviously in his own version or wording. For example, he says, "I am in agreement with every criticism Popper makes of the false transposition of natural scientific methods" (*Ibid.*: 108); in other places, Adorno elaborates on Popper's view and pushes it further: "When Popper calls the demand for unconditional value freedom paradoxical, since scientific objectivity and value freedom are themselves values, this insight is hardly as unimportant as Popper regards it" (*Ibid.*: 117). Adorno "share[s] his view" regarding psychologism with its "latent subjectivism of a value-free sociology of knowledge" (*Ibid.*: 118), but tries to expand the category of society to include certain realities that transcend the actions of individuals, so that it becomes a more meaningful category. Likewise, Adorno and Habermas continue the Hegelian–Marxist tradition that construes knowledge and logic more broadly, leaving room for non-empirical and non-testable ideas and situations, cultural phenomena and personal expressions.

Popper does not disagree with the reality of a society or a group, nor would he disagree with any rational reconstruction that expands the limits of natural phenomena or personal action (as he does with the notion of creativity, courage and passion). Instead, the concern over holistic categories, such as society or class, is a technical matter of how to study it, how to analyse it, how to empirically test theories about its behaviour as a whole which raises methodological and eventual moral problems for Popper. His situational logic and his view of methodological individualism try to solve this problem. As a number of commentators have observed, perhaps at the end of the day Popper's concern is moral more than methodological: should we punish Germany or the Nazi Party for the atrocities committed during World War II, or would it be more fruitful and appropriate to try individual leaders who murdered or who gave orders to murder innocent citizens? The Popperian approach, without explicitly saying so, is concerned with rendering collective guilt and punishment individual, with rendering personal all collective responsibility. The strength of his argument lies as much in his own methodological proposals as with his rejection of ambiguous explanatory models of history that generalize about material or ideological conditions that inevitably lead a society down this path or up another.

Situated knowledge: the feminist parallel to situational logic

In this section I examine the potential of a conjunction between two discourses, both of which are critical of science, although they use different methods of argumentation meant to move towards different goals. The conjunction of the concerns of Donna Haraway with "situated knowledge" and those of Popper in relation to "situational logic" or "problem situation" is undertaken here so as to give Popper credit for formulating ideas and methods of inquiry that are picked up in other contexts without acknowledging their intellectual antecedents.

I assume that both Popper and Haraway, in their own respective ways, are engaged in what has been loosely termed social epistemology, a concern with the view of the production and dissemination of knowledge through a network of institutional agencies, all of which are dynamically involved in the evaluation and consumption of a variety of forms of knowledge. I also assume that the social matrices used by either of them in order to contextualize their respective methodological claims are radically different; yet, despite their differences, both epistemologists deploy argumentative devices whose rhetorical force cannot remain unnoticed. As I review their views on how knowledge is situated, I will explore the similarities and differences that engender a tension in my attempt to translate their views to their respective colleagues.

In what follows I make four interrelated claims. First, in both cases engagement and concern with methodological issues (such as empiricism, rationality, criticism and objectivity) express political commitments that respond to the dominant ideology of the scientific community (e.g. the idea that scientists can police themselves or that their research is value-neutral). Secondly, Popper is a political reformer. If we view him as a conservative, then, his work nevertheless includes a radical ingredient, even if it seems to pale by comparison to Haraway's. Thirdly, Popper's contribution, however modified, can serve the feminist agenda of a successor science. Popper and Haraway display a similar concern for the establishment of an appropriate scientific methodology that supersedes Baconian inductivism as well as the strictures of logical positivism in the interest of the improvement of the human condition (however differently they view it). And fourthly, regardless of some similar epistemological concerns, the political differences between reformist Popperians and those feminists who are socialists (we may understand both in Weber's sense of *Ideal Types*) cannot and will not disappear in some dialectical *Aufhebung*.

Nowadays, claiming that one's epistemology is objective, neutral and disembodied is understood as claiming that Truth can be ascertained by divine revelation. Is Haraway's vision of the "successor science" not a throwback to something quite Popperian? I say Popperian and not logical positivist because of the distinctive characteristics of Popper's ideas that are much closer to Haraway's interest than to the ideas of any of Popper's inductivist counterparts (see below). Over the decades it has become less clear whether or not there is any sense to demarcation between induction and deduction, between rationalism and irrationalism, or between essentialism and conventionalism. Confirmation of falsifying evidence is inductive (or quasi-inductive), and the most rigorous data that conform as closely as possible to empiricism are still worded in conventional language. It is time now to examine the second of my hypotheses concerning the potential transcendence of the situation.

Haraway stands out as the most promising and problematic contemporary critic of science because she refuses to align her position with either of the two extreme camps known to us: the steadfast empiricists or the fashionable postmodernists. Instead, she tries to set up ways of validating one's scientific judgments in situation-specific circumstances so that judgments of any empirical evidence as reliable will be welcomed without thereby extrapolating from them to all judgments in all similar situations. In her words:

> So, I think my problem and "our" problem is how to have *simultaneously* an account of radical historical contingency for all knowledge claims and knowing subjects, a critical practice for recognizing our own "semiotic technologies" for making meanings, *and* a no-nonsense commitment to faithful accounts of a "real" world, one that can be partially shared and friendly to earth-wide projects of finite freedom, adequate material abundance, modest meaning in suffering, and limited happiness. Harding calls this necessary multiple desire a need for a successor science project and a postmodern insistence on irreducible difference and radical multiplicity of local knowledges. *All* components of the desire are paradoxical and dangerous, and their combination is both contradictory and necessary. Feminists do not need a doctrine of objectivity that promises transcendence, a story that loses track of its mediations just where someone might be held responsible for something, and unlimited instrumental power.
>
> (Haraway 1991: 187)

According to Haraway, then, the successor science project means this:

> Feminists have stakes in a successor science project that offers a more adequate, richer, better account of the world, in order to live in it well and in critical, reflexive relation to our own as well as others' practices of domination and the unequal parts of privilege and oppression that make up all positions. In traditional philosophical categories, the issue is ethics and politics perhaps more than epistemology. (*Ibid.*)

In this description terms such as "more adequate" and "better account of the world" appear. Their use is in order to depart from the postmodernist idiom. They have used terms such as "labyrinths" to denote their insistence that no narrative is better or worse than any other narrative as a description of reality, they are just different. In doing so, she expresses inadvertently an alliance with the Enlightenment programme that promoted progress and improvement and eventually happiness. But then she uses other terms, such as "radical historical contingency" and "semiotic technologies" that are closely associated with post-modern and Marxist rhetoric. Her sense of progress relates to "domination" and "oppression" and as such denotes a political agenda, a way in which science and technology can and should be instrumental, however defined and applied, in changing the socio-political landscape.

As one would expect from feminist critics of science, part of the complexity of the triad of epistemology, politics and ethics has to do with the power relations that pervade the scientific community and that determine its role within society. So, instead of holding on to classical ideas of epistemology and truth, science and objectivity, Haraway says: "Feminist objectivity is about limited location and situated knowledge, not about transcendence and splitting of subject and object. In this way we might become answerable for what we learn how to see" (*Ibid.*: 190). Having placed the researcher within the equation that eventually yields answers to questions we raise, Haraway goes on to say that "feminist objectivity means quite simply *situated knowledges*" (*Ibid.*: 188). What is this situated knowledge? Although *Standpoint Epistemology* is commonly associated with Sandra Harding and has its own critical literature, Haraway seems to view her version of situated knowledge in its light so that remaining focused on her version seems appropriate for my purposes. According to Haraway, "the feminist standpoint theorists' goal of an epistemology and politics of engaged, accountable positioning remains eminently potent. The goal is better accounts of the world, that is, 'science'" (*Ibid.*: 196).

Haraway, like Stephen Toulmin (1961), views the shift from the scientist as spectator to the scientist as participant, with the "units" of analysis expanding to include animated objects, as linked not only to epistemological correctness but also to an ethical awareness, political conviction and social responsibility (*Ibid.*: 198). This concern with responsibility, as we have seen in

99

Chapter 2, was introduced into philosophy by Popper and runs throughout his writing on social life as well as on the philosophy, history and methodology of science. It is the kind of contribution for which he commonly receives little credit.

How do scientists as critics go about formulating knowledge claims? No longer is it possible to assume with Bacon that observations (more precisely, observation reports) can be collected into generalizable knowledge. Nor is it tenable that science is nothing but the universal Truth. Popper says so in his tenacious attacks on inductivism, while proposing an alternative scientific method of approximating the truth through conjectures and refutations. According to Popper,

> The difference between the amoeba and Einstein is that, although both make use of the method of trial and error or elimination, the amoeba dislikes erring while Einstein is intrigued by it: he consciously searches for his errors in the hope of learning by their discovery and elimination. The method of science is the critical method.   (Popper 1979: 70)

What is this critical method? How is it applicable to all the problems that scientists study? Popper's reply is the following:

> By a situational analysis I mean a certain kind of tentative or conjectural explanation of some human action which appeals to the situation in which the agent finds himself. It may be a historical explanation: we may perhaps wish to explain how and why a certain structure of ideas was created. Admittedly, no creative action can ever be fully explained. Nevertheless, we can try, conjecturally, to give an idealized reconstruction of the problem situation in which the agent found himself, and to that extent make the action "understandable" (or "rationally understandable"), that is to say, *adequate to his situation as he saw it*. This method of situational analysis may be described as an application of the *rationality principle*. It would be a task for situational analysis to distinguish between the situation as the agent saw it, and the situation as it was (both, of course, conjectured). Thus the historian of science not only tries to explain by situational analysis the theory proposed

by a scientist as adequate, but he may even try to explain the scientist's failure. (*Ibid.*: 179)

In this sense, then, Popper's social rather than natural scientist is cast into the same role that Haraway envisions for her female and cyborg scientist. Scientific conjecture is contingent: it is in significant part historically conditioned and as such science cannot make universal, uniform claims for the truth. Once again, this is similar to the concern Haraway has over the totalizing nature of any knowledge claim and the assemblage of such claims into a successor science. As she says: "The feminist dream of a common language", be it the language of science or aesthetics, "like all dreams for a perfectly true language, of perfectly faithful naming of experience", as was the case with the introduction and application of Latin and of mathematics, "is a totalizing and imperialistic one" (Haraway 1991: 173). In the move away from totalizing explanations towards historically circumscribed ones, what is lost? What distinctive "scientific" character of knowledge claims will be abrogated? And how is this move different from that of the postmodernists, who reject all competing criteria of evaluation?

Popper, like Haraway, is worried that participant scientists might devalue the thrust of an explanation because it is "simply" historical in the sense of being a subjective claim that can be trivialized and dismissed offhand. As he says: "Thus what he has to do *qua* historian is not to re-enact past experiences, but to marshal objective arguments for and against his conjectural situational analysis" (Popper 1979: 188). To ensure some sense of objectivity, there must be a grounding that appeals *a priori* to some common social elements that go beyond the investigator or observer. For, on this both Popper and Haraway would agree: to have any political credibility and applicability, explanations must be translatable in the sense that they must be able to cross linguistic and intellectual barriers while being somewhat – not fully – indifferent to the transition, and so to the choice between some extant frameworks and presuppositions.

There is also the problem that is caused by shifting attention from the scientists to critics of science and eventually to historians of science. It makes sense to expect scientists to know the history of their field; it also makes sense for them to be their own harshest critics and see their efforts in a long line of critical assessment of their field. But must every scientist be a historian and vice versa? To quote Popper:

> The historian's task is, therefore, so to reconstruct the problem situation as it appeared to the agent, that the actions of the agent become *adequate* to the situation. This is very similar to Collingwood's method, but it eliminates from the theory of understanding and from the historical method precisely the subjective or second-world element which for Collingwood and most other theorists of understanding (hermeneuticists) is its salient point.
>
> Our conjectural reconstruction of the situation may be a real historical discovery. It may explain any aspect of history so far unexplained; and it may be corroborated by new evidence, for example by the fact that it may improve our understanding of some document, perhaps by drawing our attention to some previously overlooked or unexplained allusions.   (*Ibid.*: 189)

The investigator of whom Popper speaks here is historically informed, and reconstructs situations by adding cultural variables regardless of the "logic" of the situation. Because I find the demarcation between the sciences both problematic and contestable, I deem it helpful to consider that all the sciences are social sciences by default, areas of inquiry whose social context is or should be openly acknowledged, and thereby to consider any and all areas of inquiry susceptible to Popper's method (although he would possibly limit this to the social sciences). This is not to say that all inquiry should be reduced to the psychological elements found in the participants of the social context; rather, personal and individual decision-making processes are *post hoc* analysed rationally and reconstructed critically, so as to figure out whether this or that action was the most appropriate. According to Popper:

> The method of applying a situational logic to the social sciences is not based on any psychological assumption concerning the rationality (or otherwise) of "human nature." On the contrary: when we speak of "rational behavior" or of "irrational behavior" then we mean behavior which is, or is not, in accordance

with the logic of that situation. In fact, the psychological analysis of an action in terms of its (rational or irrational) motives presupposes – as has been pointed out by Max Weber – that we have previously developed some standard of what is to be considered as rational in the situation in question.

(Popper [1943] 1966: 97; see also Popper 1957: sections 31 and 32, on the application of situational analysis/logic to history)

Even Popper the methodologist is a sociologist of science of sorts. In his concession to the significance of social factors that establish epistemological claims and theories, Popper seems to favour the notion of situation-oriented modelling of scientific data and explanations. In this regard, his view can be also ascribed to some of his critics, the sociologists of science who have not quite read his works but assume that he is a hard-core positivist who cares only about the empirical falsification of hypotheses. For example, David Bloor of the Edinburgh Strong programme, says:

All knowledge, the sociologist could say, is conjectural and theoretical. Nothing is absolute and final. Therefore all knowledge is relative to the local situation of the thinkers who produce it: the ideas and conjectures that they are capable of producing; the problems that bother them; the interplay of assumption and criticism in their milieu; their purposes and aims; the experiences they have and the standards and meaning they apply. (Bloor 1991: 159)

Here Bloor, like others, makes common use of the term conjecture, understands it in Popper's sense of a hypothesis open to critical analysis or falsification and accepts the impossibility of any finality in epistemological terms; more astonishing, he invokes here the "local situation", the kind of situational logic Popper describes. The difference, one could claim, is this: Popper speaks of "agents" who are themselves participants in the situation whenever they decide, whereas Bloor focuses on "thinkers". But this difference, upon further reflection, dissipates as well, for all agents are thinkers, and all agents who reflect on the situation that led to their decisions immediately become thinkers. The very activity of decision-making, once stripped of its psychological elements, or once these elements are revealed with all their force, becomes open to rational reconstruction, namely, open to critical assessment. And on this the seemingly ardent critics are in full agreement.

The difference between the Popperian and feminist proposals for contextualizing epistemology remains of importance. If Haraway shifts the focus of science from epistemology to ethics and politics, is there no danger that the best one can do in a given situation is provide a personal account of the circumstances as seen by an individual? How does one formulate a political agenda that is not limited to personal pleas? Will it suffice to remain in contact with one's political community? Moreover, will the scientific appeal become (despite Popper) psychologically grounded so that one's own ego will turn out to predetermine what explanation is rendered in a specific situation?

Haraway does not want this result, nor is it a result that would buttress the claims of a feminist successor science against the criticisms of non- or anti-feminists. In her appeal she recognizes the paradox of being at once a successor and an alternative, that is, she recognizes that a multiplication of technoscientific discourses is still compatible with a marginal import of a feminist-oriented science that is supposed to replace all previous attempts, or displace them, or at least improve upon them. Must Haraway (and by extension anyone else interested in the development of a successor science) revert to the use of some form of rationality to state her case so as to appeal not only to a fragmented set of feminist critiques of science and technology?

There is no need to rehearse the critical literature concerning rationality as the logocentric basis of modern science. And so, it is crucial to recall that Popper, unlike some feminist critics, remains a steadfast rationalist, but of a different kind. He saw rationality as the way to intersubjectivity, because it is too much to expect objectivity. Would Haraway be satisfied with this epistemological grounding? Anything that would be a simple or full throwback to the masculine Age of Reason would be rejected out of hand, even when some of the issues of that Age remain important today. Still, Haraway readily concedes that "the science question in feminism is about objectivity as positioned rationality" (Haraway 1991:

196). That is, as long as rationality is qualified and redefined by feminist critics, it remains a useful tool in the hands of investigators – according to Popperians and feminists alike. But is it the same rationality? Even if not, is there a way to redefine rationality in less hegemonic or oppressive terms so as to translate (between) Popper and Haraway, or perhaps acknowledge their concerns with social and political connections from which decisions can be made?

Perhaps even a minor concession to some level of rational intersubjectivity as a political move toward a forum that permits critical evaluation and debate may illustrate the dialectical affinity between Popper and any other critic of science, feminist, and even Marxist or postmodernist. According to Agassi:

> Viewing science chiefly as purposive or as a goal-directed activity is much more in accord with the sociological approach favored by Popper, namely the rationality principle, or situational logic, or the principle of rational reconstruction. The word "rationality" in the sense of purposiveness should not be confused with "rationality" in the sense of enlightenment.
>
> (Agassi 1975: 38)

Although Agassi's interest lies with "the sense of enlightenment" that he equates with the notion of science and scientific explanation, he is in favour of relativizing rationality by contextualizing its meaning for particular purposes. While the notion of purposiveness would appeal to some feminists and other critics of science more than that of enlightenment, it is reasonable to assume that Popper was more interested in scientific enlightenment and thus found the notion of purposiveness to be a limiting case of the principle of rationality.

The notion of situational logic or the logic of situations may turn out to be the methodological or argumentative device whereby an epistemology of sorts will contain ethical and political considerations as a matter of course and not as *post hoc* additions. As such, this methodological turn may foreground the differences between critics like Popper and Haraway as opposed to whitewash them. Just because some Popperians and some feminists adopt a similar vocabulary (of situational logic and epistemology) does not mean that their use of the terms and methods will yield similar results. Why?

Ian Jarvie considers Popper's situational logic one of his most important contributions to science, even although this is the least documented of his views (found primarily in lectures, says Jarvie). Although the parameters of explanation turn on two additional principles (to that of rationality), the principle of causality (although David Hume has shown how problematic it is) and the principle of means/ends analysis, Jarvie still finds situational logic the most appropriate means with which to provide a description and prediction of an objective outcome. According to Jarvie:

> It is assumed that the situation, if objectively appraised, should favor certain means which are more effective than others and that the measure of rationality consists in the success in approaching such an "objective" appraisal. The logic of the situation, then, is an empirical description of the procedure of explanation which goes on in the social sciences; it is also a normative prescription for reform of what does not fit the description, particularly holistic and psychologistic social science; it is also, finally, a logical analysis of what underlies plausible social sciences explanations. The logic of the situation is a special case of the deductive analysis of casual explanation in general and illustrates the unity of method in the sciences. (Jarvie 1972: 4–5)

Regardless of how upbeat Jarvie sounds and despite his nostalgia for a "unity of method in the sciences" (vaguely reminiscent of the ideals of the Vienna Circle), he is willing to admit that there are some problems associated with the application of this method. In his words:

> The fundamental model for explanation in the social sciences is the logic of the situation. The logic of the situation has deeply embedded in it the rationality principle, the methodological rule that we attribute rationality – goal-directedness – to human actions in need of explanation, unless we have good grounds for not doing so. What we find problematic, and what

we find rational, are tied in essential ways to our own society
and its outlook. (*Ibid.*: 66)

Here, then, is the locus of the tension between the explanatory
model proposed by Popper and other critics, a tension that arises
in some of their own words and perhaps more noticeably in the
words of some of their critical commentators: in order to contextualize the logic of the situation an appeal must be made to culture,
to something unquantifiable and more difficult to reconstruct
rationally (because it depends on tradition or custom and habit, as
Hume calls it). But, as Fredric Jameson aptly reminds us, "in postmodern culture, 'culture' has become a product in its own right"
(Jameson 1991: x), that is, an ongoing and changing framework
that in its self-realization makes it difficult to apprehend once and
for all. Once such an appeal is made, it is no longer possible to enter
a situation as though one were in a thought experiment that provides the parameters of decision-making and a model of explanation.
The backdrop or stage is itself reconfigured as the performance
takes place. As Haraway would insist, the personal background of
oppression and discrimination, of values and ideals with which
one encounters the world and is encountered by others, constructs
one's identity in problematic ways, but ways whose difference
remains both undeniable and important. Feminists would argue
that the insertion of a (Popperian) disembodied logician, one who
admittedly is trying to avoid the pitfalls of psychologism, is so
unreasonable and untenable that it turns out to be (epistemologically) useless. As we shall see in the next chapter, Popper's
sensitivity to this predicament is not as extensive as that of the
postmodernists, since he thinks his own method has enough of a
corrective thrust to it to avoid prejudiced and biased analyses.

Some feminist critics object to Popperian situational logic as
not only too logical and too impersonal, but also as presuming
unreflectively that the definitions of rationality pertinent to particular situations are uniform with regard to some cultural background knowledge. This (political) posture belies one's confidence
that naming and defining can be done fully objectively, that is,
undertaken from an Archimedean perspective and not from the
messy perspectives of people who are engaged in the situations
that they need desperately to explain. Without those explanations

their voices would not be heard and their visions would be obscured. Incidentally, it is obvious that a similar critique can be launched against the postmodernists themselves. It has been, and we shall discuss it later.

There are other critics who complain about Popper's notion of situated logic. Williams criticizes Popper's notion of situational logic as an abstraction and a formal reconceptualization that is understood as less complex than physical situations (Williams 1989: 117). Williams says that this differentiation between the social and natural situations is wrongheaded, for there are different complexities in these contexts. This may lead Popperian researchers to reduce all social study to a deterministic and reductionist study, perhaps thereby bringing it closer to what natural scientists do, but one that does not resemble what sociologists of knowledge and science in fact do (*Ibid.*: 122ff.). According to Williams, Popper's analysis and methodological recommendation misses the importance of Bergson's ideas (from whom the term "open society" was borrowed):

> Though the terms "open society"and "closed society" apparently were used by Henri Bergson in *Two Sources of Morality and Religion*, Popper's usage is quite different. Bergson intended to capture the drama of the opening of the soul through love, philosophic reflection, and revelation of the world-wide community of man – like Eric Voeglin's "leap in being" in *Order in History*. Popper's is a thoroughly secular and rationalist distinction.   (*Ibid.*: 145)

Williams continues:

> Popper's thought in this regard lacks sympathy and the vocabulary for articulating the experience of the passage from the reality of the isolated ego or "I" to the "we" – a prerequisite, I would argue, of sustained improvement or "enlightenment" of public life in even the most liberal and individualistic of societies.   (*Ibid.*: 162)

But here we might recall an earlier quoted passage in which Popper openly talks about *passion* in the Weberian sense of a calling or a vocation, one that transcends material rewards and is undertaken for the love of it. Popper puts much stock in the sympathy, as Williams calls it, of the researcher and the emotional strife that might afflict an individual or a whole group under certain circumstances. It is in this sense that I have been arguing throughout this book about the affinity between Popper and Marx, at least in the sense that their use of scientific method, however differently they describe and ascribe it, however differently they conceptualize and apply it, is supposed to solve problems that afflict humans; theirs is not merely a theoretical exercise, but rather an attempt to alleviate (Popper) or even eliminate (Marx) the pain or suffering of individuals. So, Williams's accusation (and the feminist one along similar lines) seems convincing only if one holds on to labels that are misapplied or misrepresent the Popperian position.

Williams continues his critique also in a different vein, suggesting that despite his protestation to the contrary, Popper's analysis is broad and theoretical, abstract and logical, so that it fails to capture the individual who operates within specific social contexts, such as family dynamics, school peer pressure, etc. In short, Popper's failure at his own scientific task turns out to be an exercise in moralizing (akin, I suppose, to what has been said of Malthus's view of the disproportionate growth in population relative to the slower growth of foodstuff – and the moral is not to have sex . . .):

> As a scientific moralist, Popper thus commits the naturalistic fallacy. If we take seriously the situations in which individuals find themselves, and appreciate that they do not exclusively "maximize returns" as an Austrian economist might, but sometimes manipulate and mould, "play at" and dramatize their roles and identities as they define their situations for themselves, then Popper's deductively cumulative comparison of situations turns out to be more moralizing than a framework for empirical inquiry. To discover meaningful regularities in our social and political world, we must look at concrete and specific institutions – families, religious institutions, schools, political and economic institutions, and media of communication, to name only a few. Popper's thought seldom descends to this level of analysis.   (*Ibid*.: 182)

109

Although Williams writes about two decades after the dispute over positivism in German sociology, he seems not have gone beyond the complaints that were voiced then. The Frankfurt School, for one, maintained its epistemological position with regard to the importance of social and political institutions and the effects they have on individuals, in contradistinction to the Popperian view that the importance lies first and foremost with the individuals who give rise to and affect these institutions. It is almost the chicken and the egg: who came first? Well, the creationist says the chicken (created by God), and the evolutionist says the egg (as it evolved over time from the primeval egg, the amoeba). As we shall see in the next chapter, contextualized understanding requires that we try to make explicit the assumptions that we accept and the framework that we adopt. Likewise, the two parallel traditions in intellectual history (seen in anthropology as well as in biology and other fields of study) admit that their starting points, their baselines, differ and remain unabridged: this is where I stand, and this is what I believe, and according to my belief I construct theories and hypotheses, with explanatory and predictive power. Popper's little twist is to add: test either and then decide (rather than ask any authority which is better).

Methodological individualism

Popper begins his elucidation of methodological individualism by reference to Marx, once again, and a point of agreement (at least as a starting point) that eventually allows him to speak in his own voice. As Popper says:

> A concise formulation of Marx's opposition to psychologism, i.e. to the plausible doctrine that all laws of social life must be ultimately reducible to the psychological laws of "human nature", is his famous epigram: "It is not the consciousness of man that determines his existence – rather, it is his social existence that determines his consciousness".
>
> (Popper [1943] 1966: II, 89)

In taking off from where Marx left his anti-psychologistic view, Popper endorses two related views. First, a discussion of human nature is problematic, since there are two views concerning it, as to whether it adheres to natural or to conventional laws. Finding appropriate experiments to decide the matter, argues Popper, would be futile: "The universal occurrence of certain behaviour is not a decisive argument in favour of its instinctive character [fear of snakes], or of it being rooted in 'human nature'" (*Ibid*.: 90). So, as long as we leave human nature to be an abstract term that cannot be ascertained once and for all, we had better avoid trying to reduce the analysis of human behaviour to human nature; we must refrain from psychologism (Mill's version, as described by Popper or others).

Second, talking of social institutions – in general or relating to some particular ones, such as the market – those who follow psychologism tend to analyse them in terms of their human constituents. This would mean, in the case of the market, that we ought to consider "economic man" as an entity whose behaviour initiates and develops the behaviour of the market (see Hollis & Nell 1975). Popper quotes Mill: "The Laws of the phenomena of society are, and can be, nothing but the laws of the actions and passions of human beings" (Popper [1943] 1966: II, 91). Popper concurs with Mill's position and sees it as "one of the most praiseworthy aspects of psychologism, namely, its sane opposition to collectivism and holism" (*Ibid*.). It's in this light that Popper ends up saying:

> Psychologism is, I believe, correct only in so far as it insists upon what may be called "methodological individualism" as opposed to "methodological collectivism".   (*Ibid*.)

This is Popper's starting point, his own formulation of methodological individualism not as part of psychologism, not as a reductionist move from social behaviour to individual behaviour and then to human nature. Popper's rejection of this logic of analysis is also informed by his worry that psychologism would deteriorate into historicism, namely, look for patterns that cause or determine certain historical developments (*Ibid*.: 92). Popper claims that to some extent humans are the authors and designers of social institutions: they sometimes deliberately establish them to fulfil certain human dreams and aspirations. This fact alone delegitimates all reductionist moves every time one examines social behaviour. And yet, even those institutions "which arise as the result of conscious and intentional human actions are, as a rule, *the indirect, the unintended and often the unwanted byproducts of such actions*" (*Ibid.*: 93). It is from this point of view that Popper develops his view of situational logic described in the previous section.

If one were to reconstruct the Popperian view on methodological individualism in light of his predecessors and disciples (from Mill and Hayek to Agassi), it seems to me that two major features come to light (and which are clearly delineated by Agassi, although not in these particular terms). First, methodological individualism is an epistemological (rather than a psychological or an ontological) attempt to deal with both the problem of induction and the problem of holism. The problem of induction, as noted by Hume, describes the impossibility of ever founding certain knowledge on a collection of observable data, or the inability in principle to generalize a hypothesis or theory from a collection of particular statements (of empirical facts). In this vein, Hume also undermined the acceptance of causality as the view that every cause has a definite effect and that therefore any effect we observe can necessarily allow us in principle to discover its causes. Popper's methodological recommendation sidesteps this logical impossibility and suggests that the focus on individual cases should remain as a conjectural stepping stone from which deductions can be made, then tested and possibly refuted, and then, if needed, reformulated all over again in the light of the refutations of its earlier versions.

Likewise, holism or collectivism raised two related problems, one with regard to historicism, the view that certain developments are bound to happen in particular ways for particular reasons (causally determined), as well as the ontological question of the autonomous existence of social institutions (regardless of their origins or effects). Popper's methodological recommendation disposes of the ontological question by disregarding it, since either way certain unintended outcomes can be observed and recorded, and specific hypotheses about them can be formulated and tested, refuted and reformulated. The Marxist theory of social class, for example, seems to Popper spurious for it neither explains nor predicts the behaviour of individual workers, nor does it help solve the crises of trade cycles.

But here we are still reworking Popper's views on methodology and his attempts to provide alternatives to existing methods of inquiry (both in the natural and the social sciences). My point of departure is Agassi's brilliant summary of all the relevant positions associated with methodological individualism (Agassi & Jarvie 1987: Ch. 9). What is at stake for Popper throughout his works is freedom and responsibility. Both concepts are of course interrelated and are necessary constituents of each other. I would like to emphasize here that part of Popper's appeal to critics like me is exactly these two concepts as they are applied across disciplinary boundaries. Let us start with freedom. The freedom I have in mind is for the individual thinker and reader, researcher and student to be able to challenge anyone any time. This is disallowed in traditional societies where the elders know it all and where any expression of free thought is considered an unwelcome challenge and threat, and also in modern societies where authoritarian regimes (totalitarian and dictatorial) assume that freedom brings with it inevitable disastrous results (the breaking of norms and convention, the breaking of rules and regulations, and the breakdown of the social fabric as a whole).

But this description, if true, is not limited to such societies; it extends itself into democracies where all individuals, and not the leaders alone, are threatened by the freedom of some other individuals. Are we free to question the authority of the police or the scientific establishment? Even if we are in principle, will we be able to manifest our freedom, to actually challenge anyone? Will a beginning student find audience with the esteemed, tenured, full professor? Will the beginning researcher find audience with the esteemed, well-funded and established journal editor? So, freedom as such is not a constitutional concept or a social-contract construct, but a real problem that requires real solutions. Popper's methodological recommendations, in their simplicity (almost triviality, which I mean as a term of endearment and not condemnation), open the door for anyone to try and err, to conjecture and test and refute. This takes a lot of intellectual weight off our budding students and citizens, encouraging them to make mistakes and learn from them, rather than to avoid making mistakes and thereby avoid taking intellectual and personal risks, avoid broadening their horizons and experiment, be creative and outrageous.

Freedom is not enough. The freedom Popper promotes is not thoughtless or reckless, but both informed and responsible. If you wish to be free and independent, autonomous in your thought and action, then you had better try to appreciate the social and historical context from which and within which you operate. You had better also try to realize the extent to which your actions have consequences, some prefigured and some unintended. Popper viewed as mere copout the suggestion that nothing is your fault – since you are nothing but a product of human nature, as some Freudians say, or of the forces of society or history, as Marxists say. He loathed the Freudians and the Marxists, in their own turn, exactly for advocating these respective views. I would venture to claim that following either of them one would become less rather than more responsible; put differently, according to Popper, the Marxists and Freudians alike have a theoretical crutch on which to rest their irresponsible behaviour. And if responsibility is high on the Popperian agenda, especially around World War II, then attacking both makes more than methodological and epistemological sense; it's a moral battle cry!

The Marxists could claim, along Hegelian lines, that the march of historical development is the march of reality which in turn is the march of reason – nothing can be done about it, and it is a self-rationalizing process. We are here for the ride, and if we are very clever, we might even be self-conscious of the forces of history that underlie these processes. Capitalists, for example, cannot help themselves and are bound to be exploitive of their employees; employees cannot help themselves and are bound to be alienated. In short, this vicious circle cannot be stopped and altered; it must run its course, to use Marx's expression. Modern capitalism is bound to break down sooner or later because of its unbridled growth patterns and cycles so that excessive accumulation of wealth on the one side and increased productivity on the other would create inevitable frictions and surpluses the market place could not absorb quickly enough. The United States, then, cannot help itself and must behave like an imperial power in the late twentieth century, the way Britain did in the nineteenth century; they happen to be playing scripted roles on the historical stage. Obviously, this way of thinking requires less critical rational reflection that could provide alternatives; it requires less hard intellectual work of reflection and analysis; and it reverts to the simple principle of historical inevitability.

Surely, there are those who would object to any characterization of Marx's view of capitalism (and of Freudian psychoanalysis). Is not the Marxist portrayal of unbridled and naive capitalism in need of reconfiguration? What if capitalism as it was practised a century ago can transform itself, revise its own principles and practices, and reconstitute itself quite differently? This is something foreseen by neither Marx as a critic nor Popper as a critic and apologist. Contemporary capitalism is not what it was, and therefore the very category or label "capitalism" should be reconsidered (as I have illustrated earlier in Chapter 2). Just as "mass" was redefined from its origins in Newtonian mechanics to its Einsteinian formulation (from an absolute concept to a relative one), so must capitalism be redefined. There are as many versions of capitalism as there are societies. Those who would still insist that similar principles underlie all versions and that private property, profit maximization and the accumulation of wealth in the hands of a few still remain the basic tenets of all versions are sadly mistaken. Yes, one can find instances of exploitation, when one group takes advantage of another – but is it systematically so? Is it so by design or by default? Are there procedures and laws so as to alleviate exploitation (minimum wages, protection for safety and health, benefits that transcend hourly wages, etc.)?

Along parallel lines, Freudians could claim that one's personal and tribal background and history predetermines the psychological handicaps and potential developments to be expected. If you were abused as a child (physically, emotionally, psychologically, verbally, conceptually, environmentally, etc.), then you are bound to repeat the abuse: you will probably become an abusive person. If you were beaten or molested as a child, you are more likely to become a criminal of sorts, namely, someone who displays deviant modes of behaviour. It's your past that determines your future, and since you have no control over your past, you also have no control of what will become your future. In short, every action can be *post hoc* rationalized in this framework by eliminating the main actor or character in the narrative, the individual actor.

Here, too, one could argue about the different Freudian version of psychology and psychoanalysis. Are we all in agreement about the Freudian division of the psyche to ego, id and superego? Are we all in agreement about the ontological status of the subconscious? Even if we were, would we agree about the best methods of reaching or affecting it? What would count as a psychological experiment? Even had we agreed on this, what would count as verification as opposed to falsification? Just as my comments about capitalism above were abstract and general, I am keeping them this way here, for I refrain from going into details of Popper's critique of both and the various rejoinders to him that have appeared in the past fifty years. My concern here is not with Marxism or Freudianism as such, but with personal responsibility.

One can see, right away, why the notion of freedom and responsibility are bound up with each other. In Popper's view, the prototypical individuals according to the Marxist or Freudian lore are never free, since they are always already bound by the circumstances of their own situation and cannot free themselves from them. So, if we wish to advocate responsibility in the Popperian sense (in Agassi's version or in mine), then we are bound to insist on some sense of freedom and autonomy that can codify and illustrate, substantiate and entail one's sense of responsibility: this is my own doing and I shall be judged by it alone! I should not blame anyone but myself if I made a mistake, and try to correct it as best I can, admitting to what I have done and bearing the consequences of my actions. This becomes now an ethical stance, one which is burdensome, of course, but one which may be the motivating force behind Popper's entire edifice. Without psychologizing too much I can see how Popper the outsider, the foreigner, the misfit, wanted to be taken seriously by the establishment without compromising his integrity and his ideas, however mistaken they might be. He has been the author of his ideas, even though he gives credit to his predecessors; and he is responsible for them, and therefore he would like them to be accurately formulated and not misconstrued. The clarity of formulation so there is transparency for the detection of mistakes is itself a methodological demand that is ethical in nature: do not hide behind convoluted phrasings so that you can avoid the weight and meaning of your words.

Still, Popper's insistence on personal responsibility has an appeal that remains problematic. For example, in one of my studies I have compared the work of scientists during World War II in Germany and the United States (Sassower 1997), and commented on the well-known fact that the Germans failed to make any progress while their American counterparts (with European refugees' help) developed and detonated atomic bombs. What remained of interest, from my perspective, is the counterintuitive fact that, among researchers who worked on the bomb, the Nazi monsters afflicted no damage on their enemy, while the American freedom fighters ended up dropping atomic bombs on civilians in Japan (and not their fascist enemies in Europe). Oh, it is not a matter of science or technology, one could argue, but a matter of political and military leadership and will. Perhaps this is true. But if one were to follow the Popperian lead and focus on the individual freedom to be personally responsible for one's actions, one should reconsider this historical event from a different perspective (which incidentally happened to some of the leaders and participants of the Manhattan Project, especially to Oppenheimer). It is with this in mind that I formulated ten "suggestions" to any future scientist or engineer, researcher and student (*Ibid.*: 97–9).

I shall not rehearse them here, but simply say that one should take upon oneself the strongest sense of responsibility for the unintended consequences of one's research and study. This may entail not working on the human genome project, for example, because one cannot control research results that may wind up in the corporate world or the world of an insane dictator with enough resources to use them. What all of us fear is the unbridled behaviour of individuals; to combat this fear we can either foster strict rules and regulations and fall prey to the controls of a legal and political system that would be oppressive (relegate control to others), or demand self-control and ultimate sovereign power for the individual, but pay the price of being critical and reflective, rational and passionate – in short, being responsible.

CHAPTER 4
The predicament of applied Popperianism

In this chapter I attempt to accomplish three tasks: first, to reconnect the Popperian interest in science with the interest in social and political matters, so as to highlight the moral dimension of all his works; secondly, to highlight some parallels and overlaps between Popper's ideas and the ideas that come under the rubric of postmodernism; and thirdly, to re-examine critically the extent to which the (social) reliance on individual rationality and personal responsibility is untenable regardless of whether one relies on self-policing initiatives or legislates them within institutional confines. Pockets of success in limited communities (communes or the kibbutz movement in Palestine and then Israel) belie a structural weakness that undermines individual initiatives except under rare conditions.

The moral sense of Popperianism

Throughout this book I have repeatedly emphasized the personal historical context of Popper's work, not so much so as to highlight his biographical journey, as Jeremy Shearmur does so well (1996), but more in terms of the political environment that helped shape or influence his ideas. In doing so, I don't mean to psychologize his works or to find causal connections with, say, the conversion of his parents from Judaism but, rather, I am concerned with the role of the intellectual before and after World War II, a war that displaced thousands of intellectuals from around Europe. It seems to me that being a refugee does have an effect on one's perspective and on the point of view from which one looks at the world and the behaviour of its inhabitants. Other critics of Popper's works are in agreement with this assessment, and some, like Steve Fuller, even extend this kind of approach to include the Cold War (in the 1950s and 1960s between the United States and some of its allies and the Soviet Union and some of its allies). It is in this context that Fuller gives Popper more credit than anyone else in the intellectual community, relegating some American celebrities, like Thomas Kuhn, to the lowly and cowardly status of those who collaborated with the authorities, who were nationalists and conformists, who endorsed the "normality" of the scientific community and the academic system despite grave conditions that demanded actions and protests, courage and foresight (Fuller 2004: Ch. 16). This alludes to Heidegger the Nazi, although the similarity is severely limited, of course.

It is fascinating, as some have learned to appreciate over time, that Popper's views and personal stands were in fact more heroic and open-minded than those of others who have been heralded as relativists and pluralists, like Kuhn, as Fuller correctly observes (*Ibid.*: 10). I readily endorse his assertion: "Once Popper's philosophy of science is read alongside his political philosophy, it becomes clear that scientific inquiry and democratic policies are meant to be alternative expressions of what Popper called 'the open society'" (*Ibid.*: 16).

The way Fuller explains this point, and allows that Popper's moral horizon was more far-sighted and appropriate in the twentieth century, is always related to his damning critique of Kuhn (who interests me much less, since I never considered him to be on the same intellectual footing as Popper). In a telling point, Fuller continues to say that Popper's "'civic republican' sentiment . . . comes to the fore":

Many authoritarian regimes, especially the twentieth-century fascist and communist ones, could also persuasively claim widespread support, at least at the outset and in relation to the available alternatives. For Popper, however, the normative problem posed by these regimes is that their performance is never put to a fair test. Kuhn suffers from the same defect: a paradigm is simply an irrefutable theory that becomes the basis for an irreversible policy. (*Ibid.*: 28)

I find Fuller's account charming and heart-warming, the kind of nod or knowing smile you are fortunate to glean when an old acquaintance tells you without using one word that you have been right, that he finally gets it, that indeed the fanfare of fifty years of false adulation has come to an end, and King Kuhn is wearing no clothes!

Fuller was educated by the American establishment of philosophy of science, the so-called inductivists and positivists of the neo-Vienna Circle as well as some of their British counterparts and then the so-called sociologists of knowledge renegades. But as a recognized sociologist who moves freely across the Atlantic, he has become a convert of sorts (it is his own use of religious metaphors that brings this comment about), more favourably inclined to revisit the Popperian legacy and appreciate the kernels of truth that have never changed. These include a fierce quest for the truth with an appreciation that one never will fully attain it, a deep-seated respect for individual rights and aspirations under any and all circumstances, an ongoing suspicion of authoritarian power and conformity to any established governance or dogma, and a staunch desire to have all ideas and proposals, conjectures and hypotheses remain open to scrutiny and relentless testing, refutations and falsifications. If applied all around, this way of living and thinking, behaving and interacting would allow freedom and equality, with mutual respect and personal responsibility. Many of those who for the past few decades have been sitting on the fence in their endorsement or rejection of Popper's ideas and ideals have seen how they have withstood time (admittedly with various revisions and modifications by disciples and critics alike), as the case of Fuller exemplifies, and perhaps to a lesser extent also Stanley Aronowitz (who should have been dismissive of Popper because of his own Marxist commitments). The European tyranny of World War II has mutated into the American McCarthyism of later years and then again into some forms of extreme neo-conservatism in the UK and the USA and religious fanaticism in other parts of the world (and at times in the western world as well) in more recent years.

Popper's own concerns with the differences he wanted to highlight in the case of Socrates and Plato – namely, emphasizing the primacy of the individual as an independent agent who can eschew any formal governance whatsoever (except some minimal respect for others) as opposed to fitting well and fulfilling one's prescribed destiny within a prefigured social and political organization (the *Republic* or the Soviet State) – are neither original nor radical. In fact, there are many scholars whose own ideological convictions vary from each other, such as Leo Strauss (Strauss & Cropsey 1972) and Sheldon Wolin (2004), who show in their respective collections and surveys that this has been a perennial issue for any political philosopher concerned with the political settings most appropriate for the enhancement of individual freedom and social equality. Wolin, for example, complains about Popper's focus on liberalism (the nineteenth-century variant) with little regard to democracy as such and the material conditions under which it can prosper. Likewise, he faults Popper for dealing too abstractly with the notion of "problem solving" as a methodological battle-cry and ideological mantra while refusing to address directly specific problems that plagued his days. And finally, Wolin is frustrated with the fact that although Popper was directly affected by World War II and the Cold War, his own pronouncements remain quite elusive and remote from those devastating occurrences even in his notorious *Open Society and Its Enemies* (Wolin 2004: 495–503). I shall return to some of these complaints in the last section of this chapter, where I explain the predicament of Popper's legacy.

Many political historians and philosophers fail to cast their net wide enough to collect the works of intellectuals and artists that critically engage political and ideological matters but from a different perspective or with a different approach. For example, there are many European intellectuals, like Bertrand Russell (1949), who in the post-war years wrote extensively about the fine line or balance that ought to be drawn or between "authority" and the "individual". Some of these public intellectuals transformed the arguments into fiction, like George Orwell (in both his famous texts of 1946 and 1949), realizing that the warnings of earlier generations of intellectuals were both warranted and insightful (see especially Orwell's unacknowledged debt to Zamiatin's *WE* [1924]!). These were thinkers and academics, authors and artists, who felt compelled to say something (their way of doing something) in order to thwart another fascist threat to freedom or another political catastrophe; these were the thinkers who believed that their words could make a difference and that they had a moral obligation to speak out (in a way that has never been shared by their American counterparts; perhaps this is so since no twentieth-century war was fought on American soil).

Whether Russell and Orwell, for example, were more worried about the horrors of Stalinism or some other regime of their time is less important for assessing Popper's work, for he can be seen as a public intellectual as well who found a receptive audience once in a while (with his *Open Society*) around the academy, and who realized how his ideas about science and politics were in fact intertwined: the freedom to protest and criticize should be equally exercised in any part of our life (and not limited to course work at the university, for example). Censorship is morally unacceptable not only because it is wrong to silence the voices of others (who should have the right of freedom of speech no matter what they say), but also because it impedes the progress and growth of knowledge (scientific and political alike). For the Vienna Circle founders and the likes of Kuhn later on, such unbridled openness is threatening to the "paradigm" that has been established (namely, verified, confirmed) and from which they all benefit (intellectual security, academic positions, grant awards). Suggesting that non-scientists should be able to critically assess the research of scientists flies in the face of the claims of expertise (see Sassower 1995), but in fact upholds a basic moral principle of *prima facie* equality among all human beings (and their potential to grasp the ideas of others – itself an Enlightenment ideal that propelled public education in the western world – and offer tests according to which they can be judged). So, without religious fanfare or pretence, one can find in Popper's methodological recommendation all the moral principles one needs for establishing democratic institutions and interpersonal relationships. No wonder the likes of George Soros (mentioned earlier in Chapter 2) have found inspiration in Popper or have used Popper as the justification for their own ideas about pedagogy and democracy in central Europe after the fall of the Berlin Wall in 1989.

As younger intellectuals finally realize, Popper's legacy is about timing as well! It matters when you say what you say and to whom; the context makes a difference! Heidegger said much that might have been important before the National Socialists came to power in Germany and too little once they ruled with an iron fist; Kuhn, too, said too little during the Cold War to protect the ideals of freedom, and let his ideas of "normal science" and the "appropriate" dominance of the scientific establishment rule the day (in the hands of university administrators and politicians, as Fuller convincingly explains). Popper, for one, spoke up and was ridiculed, ostracized by his peers and other intellectuals, and considered an old-fashioned conservative reactionary despite his own words and deeds to the contrary. I am not trying to defend him and his thought, for he needs no defence; nor am I trying to rehabilitate his reputation, since he never really lost it (unlike Heidegger who needed Hannah Arendt, of all people, to vouch for him and grant him intellectual licence to practice in the United States after he was banned from teaching in Germany). Instead, I am reflecting on my own ambivalence with Popper's ideas and works, having found in him the perverse inspiration as a young graduate student because he was not the "cool" philosopher or thinker to whom everyone was flocking. Popper?, they would ask with mild amusement and repulsion, you must be kidding! These were the days in Boston when Thomas McCarthy was translating Jürgen Habermas and suggesting that the second coming was revealed in our confused midst, silencing any dissent in the name of communicative rationality and the legacy of the neo-Marxist Frankfurt School with a Weberian twist.

World War II and the Cold War were over; the scars of Vietnam and the glory of the Civil Rights movement were over, too. What was left? Marx was soon to be replaced by Nietzsche as the preferred stock reference to quote in one's texts, and existentialism of a new kind was to replace both orthodoxy and nihilism. Is Popper an orthodox dogmatist of the positivist strand or an existential nihilist of the European tradition? Is he simply a European pragmatist in the James, Peirce, Dewey mould, or an enigmatic provocateur? If Popper's students are any indication of his influence on their thought and works, not to mention their personal communicative disposition in conferences and in print, then all of the above hold true – from the introspective to the outrageous, from the mild compromiser to the radical critic. His critical disciples are as different from each other as can be imagined, and this is what simultaneously gives the Popperian clan its force and weakness, its continued potency and its utter irrelevancy. There might be a Popperian ethos but not a Popperian "School"; there might be a Popperian legacy, but not a Popperian "Movement" or "Programme". In short, there is, as he wished all along, a lasting impact on individual thinkers, and even a new mind-set of the intellectual culture as a whole, but not a school.

Perhaps what is missing from the appreciation of Popper's legacy is the underlying moral character of what he said and wrote. Perhaps this is missing because unlike Kant, Popper never wrote a treatise on morality as such. Instead, he wrote about science and society, about people and institutions, about the need to inject more morality into political practice, and about cognitive processes and social policies in ways that could be understood in moral terms with a great deal of sensitivity to the individual participants. Like Aristotle, who wrote about friendship as a foundational concept in ethics, so Popper wrote about individual autonomy and responsibility as foundational concepts in science. Neither ignored social and political institutions, but both appreciated the extent to which an appeal must be made first and foremost (and perhaps even in the last analysis) to those who compose these institutions, those who operate them and practise their trades within them, and appeal to them personally to remain virtuous in some sense of the term. Each one of us is a moral entity and a potential role model to others; each one of us embodies a set of values that are expressed implicitly and explicitly in everything we do on a daily basis. To forget this and hold on to (or hide behind) a set of commandments or a set of religious beliefs is cowardice and lack of self-conscious reflection; this goes against the plea to be a critical rationalist and a responsible citizen.

Popper and postmodern technoscience

To describe postmodern technoscience we must describe technoscience first and then postmodernism and in both cases find the ways in which Popper could fit these ideas (be they definitions or classifications). "Technoscience" is a late twentieth-century term that Jean François Lyotard introduced and Stephen Toulmin used as early as the 1970s to describe the inter-relatedness and mutual dependence of science and technology. A few of us still insist on this coinage, keeping a keen eye on the substance behind the term, rather than on a desire to reformulate terms (science and technology) that could be just as useful. Instead of understanding technology as applied science and science as the theoretical foundation of technological developments (as Popper has), there has been an appreciation of the rich historical record (as in the case of Pierre Duhem) in which technological innovation leads to scientific breakthrough, and in which scientific theories can only be tested and reformulated because of engineering insights (as Agassi has been arguing for three decades). I shall come back to this issue later.

Postmodernism incorporates at least the following three elements. First is the denial of any privileging whatsoever, so that any claim or principle or idea or theory is on a par with any other. No matter what their origins and current credibility are, they ought to have their day in the intellectual courts. Secondly, it is the insistence on the fluidity of adherence to tradition, so that pre-modern, modern, a-modern, and postmodern methods of inquiry should all be consulted and incorporated into the knowledge framework on which decisions are to be based. This means, for example, that romantic ideals are not contrasted with those of the Enlightenment rationalists but viewed as interwoven with them. And thirdly, it is the refusal to rest all ideas and observations, all claims and theories, on one set of foundations, one set of principles. In this sense, then, postmodernists insist on contextualizing judgments to particular frameworks and settings so that when something is judged the appropriateness of the criteria by which it is judged will be open to examination as well.

This brief summary does injustice to the many variants of postmodernism that it ignores, and to the many variations of these three themes. Nor does it account for the artistic and architectural antecedents of the movement, whether Robert Ventura is mentioned or others (for more on this see Hoesterey 1991). The French and the American prototypes differ in many respects, and discerning the differences between them would not further my discussion here. Likewise, there are those who still insist that there isn't such a thing as postmodernism: either it is a reincarnation of some forms of Romanticism or it is a faddish misconception whose fashionable acceptance is politically irresponsible and epistemologically misguided. Even among its most familiar advocates, postmodernism has been mocked, derided and critically presented. Here is Lyotard:

Is postmodernity the pastime of an old man who scrounges in the garbage-heap of finality looking for leftovers . . . and who turns this into the glory of his novelty, into his promise of change? (Lyotard [1988] 1990: 136)

Yet, despite this line of questioning and self-doubt, I wish to plead for some sensitivity to the salient points one can glean from this way of doing business. Furthermore, I wish to argue that Popper, the alleged conservative empiricist, the metaphysical realist with an approximation of the Truth and the strict rationalist, does exhibit postmodernist symptoms in every chapter of every book he has ever written. Moreover, postmodernists deploy Popper's insights and are influenced by his contributions without giving him the credit that is his due. Having said this, I do not mean it in the trite sense that anyone's words and ideas might contain in them the seeds of postmodern gestures or critical rationalism. Rather, I mean it in a more weighty sense that to be postmodern in relation to anything scientific, for example, is to be a critical rationalist in the tradition of Popper, Agassi and Jarvie. That is, to be critical of the scientific establishment is a social, political, economic and moral posture that lowers the threshold for debate and dismisses the gatekeepers, and always recognizes that the best we can accomplish is to deal with multiple truths (small "t" and plural).

For example, think of Popper's landmark recommendation to try to provide conjectures and then try to falsify them: is this not a way to ignore all privileges? Is he not advocating the egalitarian principle of listening to every conjecture, however foolish, and allowing anyone, however meek, to refute it? Is he not an old-fashioned liberal champion of equal opportunity to all efforts to conjecture and falsify? Amidst the rich history of the aristocratic engagement with and subsidy of the sciences in the United Kingdom (since Bacon's days), attention was paid to outsiders and foreigners, even Jews, as possible contributors to the advancement of learning (and eventually to the sciences). Likewise, it was Popper who reminded us to go back to the pre-Socratic thinkers so as to bolster his methodological proposals. Juxtaposing ancient Greek ideas on to the context of twentieth-century philosophy of science was adventurous and bold. It was a journey similar to the one he took when examining the history of political ideas in order to formulate his principles of an open society. Old ideas were treated with the same care as the new, re-examining their currency against a tradition that accepted them as if no reinterpretations were ever warranted, and this was a novel and fruitful approach. And finally, although one could find a reductionist gesture and a heavy-handed leaning towards a rationalist foundation in all of his works, Popper is still the one speaking of putative truths and not of the absolute Truth. He is still claiming that the process of approximating truths we might never fully know is itself a worthwhile and epistemologically significant process in the name of the progress of the sciences.

Some earlier disciples and critics timidly use the term "postmodern" in passing when commenting on Popper. One is Jeremy Shearmur, who suggests that "the younger Popper and postmodernism share a rejection of historical teleology. With this I am in full agreement" (Shearmur 1996: 2). Similarly, even a plain and unassuming survey of Popper's views by Mark Notturno, repeatedly invokes his philosophical insights and innovations in what I may suggest are quite postmodern terms. For example, Notturno says:

> Popper used to tell his students that he proposed falsifiability as the logic of scientific discovery in an effort to replace Science with a capital "S" with science with a small "s": that he wanted, in other words, to show that science is a human affair, and a highly fallible affair; that scientists make mistakes just like everyone else, and perhaps even more than other people because they have more opportunities to make them; that the best we can do in science is to try and eliminate our errors; and, most important, that there is no such thing as a Scientific Knowledge that can speak *ex cathedra*.
>
> (Notturno 2003: 2)

Popper's project was not "Foundationalist", Notturno continues to explain, since he refused to play the game of justification, namely, the process by which one bolsters or shores up one's ideas and theories, trying to claim rationality and objectivity for them beyond the specific incidents in which their rational and objective character can be tested and revised, reformulated and retested

(*Ibid.*: 7). Similarly, Notturno finds other ways to distance Popper and his ideas from the positivism of his age and from the quest for a Foundation that historically characterized much of the European philosophical tendencies (all the way through Kant and the Enlightenment leaders). He suggests that, unlike the positivism of the Vienna Circle, Popper's proposal of falsifiability differs from their own verifiability in the sense that for them it was a criterion of meaning (especially as a measure to discard metaphysics and other meaningless statements that could not be empirically confirmed), while for him it was rather a "normative proposal about what we should and should not regard as scientific" (*Ibid.*: 19–20).

Time and again, Notturno takes Popper to have been the voice of reason in the midst of stubborn reductionism, a conciliatory voice that always insisted on the tentative nature of any inquiry (scientific included). Popper is the one who sounds the voice of the non-conclusiveness of all data, no matter how empirically robust they are, and the ongoing search for truth with a small "t", just as we remain engaged in science with a small "s". It is this explicit admission that renders the Popperian legacy postmodern, with a great deal of humility and openness, a great deal of respect for pluralism on any level of inquiry as Fuller submits and as Agassi and Jarvie, for example, practise when they discuss a variety of anthropological topics from magic and superstition to tribal traditions and folklore. If one were to take postmodernism for its methodological recommendations and appreciate its obliteration of the rigid confines of modernism, then the comments of many of Popper's critics sound very much like my own in so far as Popperians and at least some postmodernists have much more in common than may meet the eye on a superficial glance through second-hand reports and surveys. Although my own interest might be more explicit and bold, it seems to follow a path already charted a decade ago.

Of course, some would argue against everything said so far about the affinity of Popper to the postmodern way of thinking (see Agassi 1991). For some, Popperian rationalism is anathema to what seems to be postmodern irrationalism; to others it would be the way in which for Popper there are clear criteria by which to choose among competing theories while the postmodernists seem to let anything be equal in meaning and importance to anything else (in Feyerabend's sense of methodological anarchism, 1975). But before we continue this line of fruitless comparison, it might be more fruitful to tease out those elements that do have some similarity and find some affinity between the two ways of thinking so as to translate and bridge between intellectual gaps. The intellectual benefit from this is obvious: what the two parties share in common they need not debate between themselves any more (and instead they can focus on their differences). Yet the reason for doing so is still pressing and is more political than epistemological for two reasons. First, it would underscore the fact that every epistemological conviction and choice belies a political or ideological commitment of sorts, at least in the Popperian sense of showing readiness to try to solve problems rather than set parameters for inquiry as such; and secondly, it would create alliances and provide a more fertile critical landscape in which to cultivate new ideas so as to solve social, political, economic and moral problems that arise from time to time. So, even if we agree that postmodernists like Lyotard have an affinity with Popper and his ideas to the extent that they use rational means by which to make their points and that they all believe in the value of critique, there is a contested issue at hand: relativism (in the sense of non- or anti-foundationalism). It is this issue that brings Popper's ideas to the brink of my stretched comparison.

If relativism is traditionally contrasted with objectivity and absolutism, and if relativism is associated with postmodernism, and if relativists are accused of being irrational in their choices of criteria of demarcation and decision-making, then how can anyone in his right mind bring Popper close to this way of thinking? Perhaps the answer has more to do with the kind of relativism associated with postmodernism as opposed to recasting Popper's ideas in a relativist framework. Perhaps we also need to loosen the sense of "objectivity" that is attributed to Popper, since he and some of his former students were more inclined to use the (Kantian) softer notion of inter-subjectivity rather than some absolute objectivity. This, incidentally, is a recurring theme for Popper when he discusses conventionalism as a view that depends on its social matrix and is not at all arbitrary or irrational in, say, the Kuhnian sense (Popper 1959: Ch. II). Perhaps Lyotard's questions about the Holocaust can help highlight some of these concerns.

If one were to adhere to Lyotard's postmodern injunction to judge everything case by case, that is, to contextualize every set of conditions and provide the criteria according to which they ought to be assessed, then we will be unable to appeal to some over-arching principles or foundations. We would be unable, then, to condemn the horrors of the Nazis categorically (in Kant's sense). In short, one could find oneself in the position of being unable to condemn the Holocaust. The Holocaust must be condemned – but according to what principles? What objective and universal principles could be agreed upon? And surely the facts of the matter, namely, the horrible reality of Auschwitz and its gas chambers, must be faced. As Lyotard answers:

> But, with Auschwitz, something new has happened in history . . . the facts, the testimonies . . . the documents . . . and the names, finally the possibility of various kinds of phrases whose conjunction makes reality, all this has been destroyed as much as possible. (Lyotard 1988: 58)

Following Fackenheim, Lyotard admits that "Auschwitz is the most real of realities in this respect" (*Ibid.*: 58). As a label to a whole discourse of the Holocaust, Auschwitz suspends and empties the speculative elements of language and its interpretive ambiguities (*Ibid.*: 88). The facts and testimonies, the observa-tional reports scientists worry about and continue to contest take on a new meaning in the case of the Holocaust. Can the facts of the termination of six million Jews be challenged? Of course they can. Can the Holocaust be substantiated? And if it can, then by what methods? Are the criteria themselves universal or sub-jective? What status and legitimacy should we give to survivors? Should we apply the criteria of the Royal Society and, if yes, are they the criteria that Bacon has provided, or are they those of the Vienna Circle?

Before we know it, we slipped from the esoteric debates of the academic community (about empiricism and rationalism, meth-odology and epistemology) to the front-page news and popularity of Spielberg's *Schindler's List*. Where do facts end and the fictions begin? If a movie maker could set a stage with gas chambers – a fictionalized rendition of unimaginable acts of human humiliation and destruction, why not claim that the whole affair was nothing but a Jewish fiction (or conspiracy) to solicit sympathy and destroy the good reputation of National Socialism? Besides, if relativism should determine everything from ontology to epistemology and metaphysics, then why not listen only to the narratives of the Nazis and accept their right of national eugenics? As with any kind of representation, as Lyotard reminds us, "representing 'Auschwitz' in images and words . . . must remain unrepresentable" (1990: 26).

In order to answer these questions, and in order to modify his general endorsement of the view of contextualizing decisions and assessing the criteria by which they are made, Lyotard came up with his view of Auschwitz. He used the Holocaust as the litmus test for the cavalier reinterpretation of language, facts, and the reality they attempt to describe. And then, any postmodern critique would stand or fall depending on its ability to condemn the Holocaust, to show that no matter what context or what language game one were to use, the ethical dimension of such a reality would become clear no matter who observed or when it was observed. And here Popper and Lyotard could come closer to each other's views, especially in light of the earlier discussion (in Chapter 3) about situational logic (which is at once rational, critical and contextual). But do they?

Some would say that if Lyotard is a relativist, then he fails his own test for he must either uphold standards, foundations, or a set of moral principles, or relinquish any such appeal. If he is not a relativist, after all, then he is already in the rationalist camp, possibly the Popperian kind, and then obviously their views are close. So, perhaps the more precise phrasing of any reasonable description of the possible affinity between these thinkers' ideas should be this. Although their starting points and convictions seem diametrically opposed on the face of it, once they examine some difficult situations and pieces of reality, they find themselves making metaphysical compromises that bring them closer together no matter what their starting points were. Popper moves towards contextualization without relinquishing his adherence to rationality and critique, and Lyotard moves towards a rational assessment of the criteria by which the contextual of situations are judged without relinquishing his case-by-case methodology and epistemology.

Although Popper does not address the Holocaust directly in his philosophical discussions of science and its progress (unless one considers his interview comments about the atomic bomb to be relevant here; Popper 1999), and although Popper allows a great deal of latitude to the veracity and ultimate credibility of any claim (as long as it remains open to testing and refutation), his method remains critical and rational – it probes while remaining sceptical; it conjectures while inviting falsification; it suggests examining the logic of the situation (as we have seen in the comparison with Haraway's situated knowledge above). It is exactly in this sense of openness that the Popperian legacy informs the postmodern turn (however nascent it may be throughout the history of ideas, as Lyotard alludes). Lyotard relies on reality and refuses to deny it (unlike some more radical social constructivists on the British Isles or their French counterparts). He worries that without the testimonies of survivors and the truths associated with their memories of sufferings, the very facts of the Holocaust would be challenged. In short, Lyotard worries about the political and ethical consequences of poorly or inappropriately applying the postmodern insights, or ignoring empirical facts and observations in the name of the fictional nature of constructing reality. Assuredly, Popper and Lyotard are metaphysical realists!

The moral of the story, then, is threefold. First, epistemological pronouncements are political in the sense that they belie antecedent ideological commitments and have political consequences. Put differently, there is a short distance between the philosophy of science and the Holocaust (whether we speak of eugenics, facts and observations, reality, meaning, memory or truth). Secondly, the refusal to appeal to ultimate principles or reduce all knowledge claims to one static foundation is not a refusal to make a reasonable appeal to guidelines and criteria of judgement that are historically and socially informed. As long as the appeal remains open-ended and invites ongoing criticism and revisions, then there is hope that some progress in improving the human condition will take place (because the discourse or debate itself will be rational and would enhance the quest for truth without violence). And thirdly, being a philosopher (whether of science or of history) without appreciating the ethical dimension of every intellectual choice one makes is to do injustice to the very notion of being a philosopher. Popper's open society, as we have seen so far, is not limited to the political arena, but extends to the scientific community. I wish at times he would have extended it to the academic community so as to test the applicability and efficacy of his ideas, and to put the kind of moral pressure on the behaviour of academic administrators and faculties, so that they would take the high moral road in comparison to politicians and corporate managers, military leaders and bureaucrats.

Both Popper and Lyotard, in their different ways, acknowledged the intimate relationship between science and power, not in Bacon's original sense of "mastering nature", but in the frightening and more contemporary sense of the military–industrial complex, where technoscientific knowledge is appropriated by corporate giants and sold to the highest national interest. I shall work through some of Lyotard's statements in order to illustrate how the Popperian legacy seeps through in a much more profound and subtle way than commonly recognized. It is not that I wish to turn Popper into a postmodernist nor the postmodernists into Popperians. Instead, the point is that Popper's legacy is more pervasive than we admit to ourselves; this pervasiveness is an indication that something useful has been said; and the usefulness of the Popperian legacy can be gleaned in numerous areas of intellectual and scientific research.

In Lyotard's terms, we can observe the concern with knowledge in general and scientific knowledge in particular in the following way: "Knowledge in the form of an informational commodity indispensable to productive power is already, and will continue to be, a major – perhaps *the* major – stake in the worldwide competition for power" (Lyotard [1979] 1984: 5). Sure enough, Lyotard echoes Popper's insight about the validity of knowledge, the shift from validation through verification to validation through falsification. Of course, unlike Popper, he pushes his point to the level of self-legitimation, a process by which one declares the validity of one's work based on the work itself:

A statement of science gains no validity from the fact of being reported. Even in the case of pedagogy, it is taught only if it is still verifiable in the present through argumentation and proof. In itself, it is never secure from "falsification". (*Ibid.*: 26)

Now, self-legitimating statements and declarations are not as outlandish as they may sound at first, and they have been historically used quite successfully – as can be witnessed with the American Declaration of Independence: the appeal was to itself, not to the gods or other nations and their constitutions. But to declare independence to gain freedom is different from declaring self-legitimation as a power play, as a way to consolidate power in the hands of a few wealthy patrons or political leaders.

Worrying about the complicity of scientists with those who fund their research, Lyotard suggests that: "Scientists, technicians, and instruments are purchased not to find truth, but to augment power" (*Ibid.*: 46). What allows this process to continue unhampered is the fact that the laws of the land provide a powerful mechanism for the self-legitimation of science at least in terms of its efficiency and productivity (*Ibid.*: 47). This process is worrisome to the same extent that Popper worried about making statements bold enough and conjectures transparent enough that they would be open to criticism and testing from outside the scientific community, whether the solutions they proposed worked out in practice, for example, or failed miserably. The power garnered by scientists and their funding agencies also worried Popper to the extent that he demanded an open society that would encourage public scrutiny and access to all newcomers (so that an elite group would not be able to control the scientific enterprise).

When speaking of the scientific "game" which has validity no more and no less than other discursive games, Lyotard comes back to Popper's concern with one's responsibility, all the way to a tacit agreement that the individual scientist be made responsible for actions undertaken in the name of "science". In Lyotard's words: ". . . it makes the 'players' assume responsibility not only for the statements they propose, but also for the rules to which they submit those statements in order to render them acceptable" (*Ibid.*: 62). The so-called scientific game itself cannot be a responsible agent in the way that an individual can be, so the postmodern critic, more than the neo-Marxist, Frankfurt-School one, ends up upholding the primacy of individual accountability. Yes, there are many critical commentators that find the postmodern stance to be politically naive and even uninformed (see, for example, Guattari 1986). But in this context, and especially in the case of Popper and

Lyotard, I find two great thinkers who have an ethical concern that runs deep through their respective theories and frameworks for discussion. They are haunted by the European experiences of the twentieth century, and they see themselves as public intellectuals whose own commentary must be explicitly normative (rather than be implicitly embedded in their writings and eventually teased out by others).

I would venture to suggest that in both sets of writings we can find the following underlying questions: Are we willing to invite criticism and change our views in every arena? Do we assume that rationality of some sort could be the common ground on which to hold our debates? Are we interested in applying insights from one arena to another? Are we committed to improving the human condition? I would even translate some of these more general questions into more humble but direct ones: Are we welcoming junior faculty and students to falsify our statements and opinions and expose our mistakes? I guess the answer is probably not enough for either Popper or Lyotard, since we wish to maintain our authority and seniority, and hide our ignorance and insecurity.

The Popperian predicament

Some of the lessons we have learned from the previous century had to do with politics and not so much with science, unless we appreciate the extent to which the scientific enterprise is not merely a tool in the hands of politicians (to promote patriotism, as was the case in going to the moon) but in fact determines political choices (as with the atomic bomb, for example). More importantly, as Popper's legacy makes abundantly clear, methodological questions regarding the history of science were answered in politically significant ways, as they were politically loaded, so to speak. The idea that celestial movements are supposed to adhere to divine will and that biological developments conform to God's plans are themselves political ideas that granted religious authorities the power they demanded. Anything outside the biblical realm (as strictly interpreted by church bureaucrats) was suspect because it was potentially critical, and anything critical was suspect because it was potentially threatening and destructive of the religious edifice as dogmatically canonized by the church (as Spinoza learned all too well, being excommunicated twice). It is from this perspective that I laud everything Popperian: being non-religious and critical, being almost recklessly critical to the point of eschewing any and all authority, so that all we have left is the courage and integrity of the individual.

Oh yes, Popper shields the courageous individual from the pitfalls of relativism (anything goes, and anything is as good as anything else) and nihilism (it does not matter what you say or do since we are all bound to die soon). In his own battle with the Establishment of the scientific community, the state authorities, and the industrial–military complex, he exemplifies a certain heroic stance that might be too much to stomach. Perhaps his recommendation is so idealized, so far-fetched, that it loses its appeal as a heuristic (a useful ideal towards which one should strive even if it can never be reached) or an ideal (in Weber's sense of an *Ideal Type* against which one measures one's own reality and accomplishments). Perhaps his idealized vision is applicable only to the rare cases of individuals whose privileged position permits them to take risks and not be exiled or destroyed, because the worst that can happen to them is temporary ridicule and loss of social standing.

But before we continue to examine the so-called bourgeois context within which individual courage can flourish, we should recall some experiments (other than in the Soviet Union) where communal interaction could lead to creativity and critical assessment of decision-making processes with mutual respect. This theme, incidentally, runs through Shearmur's book on Popper's political thought in which the Kantian notion of humans as ends and not as means comes to light (Shearmur 1996: Ch. 1). Of course, as Shearmur and others contend, Popper's social engineering, his piecemeal process for improving upon solutions to social problems is promising only under certain conditions that some would argue remain untenable. For example, what kind of human nature must one presuppose in order to allow a smooth and conflict-free progress towards social change? Under what material and social conditions would it be possible to convince those upholding radically different views to collaborate or put aside their differences? Although theoretically appealing, one wonders how practical these suggestions are. Put differently, Popper's suggestions are considered problematic also by his admirers and former students, those who believe that the focus on individualism is a moral one and not simply methodological.

Since I have tried to show throughout this book the affinity between Popper's ideas and those of Marx and the feminists and the postmodernists, and since I have tried to take his ideas outside their historical or limited confines in philosophy of science textbooks and manuals, I would like to explain why this makes sense by the twenty-first century. To begin with, we must agree that one's biography does have an impact on one's thinking, so that a refugee with Jewish lineage is bound to be critically disposed to the ideas that run his culture and make him suffer (more on this in Hacohen 2000). Secondly, we must acknowledge that Popper's intellectual output measures well against many others in the history of ideas (Kant comes to mind right away), to the extent that it covers a variety of topics and areas of research, and therefore it would be unfair to focus on only one facet while ignoring all others (as methodologists of science often do). Thirdly, since Popper has an extremely wide range of interest, we must look for and recognize some underlying themes that bind his works; perhaps there is a thread with which to connect them all (for example, the call for individual freedom and responsibility). Fourthly, even although Popper's insistence on individualism might sound similar to the reductionism of socio-biologists and psychologists (or game theorists), it might be more appropriate to think of him as an existentialist who worries about the human condition and the spirit of creativity. And finally, whatever demons Popper fought and however misinformed or uninformed he might have been (about the Soviet Union's threat, for example, or the Cold War), he fought them openly and bravely, being painfully clear what he was afraid of and what he hoped could be accomplished. So, his own mistakes could be ascertained right away, tested and improved upon (rather than hushed or defended). This is more than can be said about most intellectuals who refuse to speak out and become public intellectuals and engage in the affairs of the state.

Perhaps Popper's legacy is jewish (in the lower case 'j') and therefore he poses more questions than answers to his disciples and critics. By jewish I mean the sense of loss, on the one hand, that every Jew is bound to feel culturally as a member of a displaced community ("the wandering Jew"), and the commitment to disputation ("for the greater glory of God"), on the other. Being the perennial outsiders, the jews are adept at critically engaging the community into which they are exiled, wherever they find refuge from persecution. While doing so, assimilation is always tempting, but the jews can't help being critical, even self-critical. In order to be understood, the jews must be rational so that rational discourse itself (regardless of the language one uses) remains universal and can be understood or translated across cultural boundaries. And finally, the jews endorse the focus on the individual because each of them wants to be considered as different from the group, as being uniquely worthy of personal consideration, on the one hand, and they appreciate how collective guilt, on the other hand, inadvertently could let criminals avoid personal guilt and punishment.

My characterization of Popper's legacy in Jewish terms might seem bizarre, even ludicrous, given his own European assimilation. But this is exactly the predicament that lies at the heart of Popper's legacy: he is both a conservative and a liberal, an openminded critic and rigorous task-master who is steeped in the Enlightenment tradition, a refugee and a knighted British subject, a famous intellectual and forgotten footnote, a champion of an objective reality and a compassionate existentialist. So, will the "real Popper" please appear? The predicament is that there are many views covered by Popper, and that in many cases they were tailored, as he repeatedly insisted, to solve specific problems. It is in this sense that his situational logic is contextualized and limited by its own declared confines. It is in this sense that he can remain a moralist but be focused more narrowly than, say, Kant. It is also in this sense that his personal surroundings looked more like those of elitist and privileged thinkers than the ones he seems to be promoting, the free-thinkers who roamed the *agora*, like Socrates. Perhaps it is all about style. Socrates, Popper's favourite role model, chatted with acquaintances and gently prodded them along his argumentative and dialectical lines. Popper, by contrast, was a harsh conversationalist who had no patience for sloppy thinking and poorly phrased statements, and he preferred to rewrite his thought endlessly so as to be as careful and clear about what he meant. Socrates was a midwife of ideas, while Popper was the high priest who would christen them if he found them worthy. Perhaps this is a matter of temperament, perhaps a psychological disposition. Perhaps Socrates was established enough to afford losing his intellectual battles and exchanges and risk his life for his beliefs, while Popper felt always under siege and worried about survival. It is hard to say what goes on in people's minds, as Popper tells us, unless there are tests (crucial experiments, if you wish) that can determine clearly, even if not once and for all, that this or that hypothesis is mistaken. I do not know what tests Popper's ideas should undergo, except to say that his ideas have weathered fairly well in almost one hundred years: some of them still resonate with us today and remain useful warnings against authority (scientific and political alike), dogma (of others and our own), complacency (about what we know), comfort (as members of groups and associations, organizations and communities), and irresponsibility (of our own actions and those of others).

My own lessons from having read Popper's works for the past twenty years have to do with working hard on the life of the mind. This means, among other things, learning from history how trial and error moved us in unexpected ways and appreciating the interpretive element in any historical report, maintaining my integrity and honesty by disclosing my own ignorance and demanding the same of others, allowing myself to be corrected by others and expecting others to do the same, and being responsible for my intellectual statements as potentially powerful tools and requiring everyone else to adopt the same attitude. This, of course, is at times a lonely road, at times a depressing way to lead one's life, and only seldom a road that brings the kind of Spinozist reward, peace of mind.

Perhaps one cannot learn any of this and must be predisposed to have a character both strong and malleable enough to be able to handle this way of life. Perhaps we cannot teach intellectual courage the way we try and teach courage in the battlefield. It might be this realization that drove Popper to set many of his debates and controversies with others as battles that demanded personal courage and sharp weapons, clearly defined goals, and a sense of victory or defeat. Could he have thought that only with this kind of parallel he could induce a sense of urgency and seriousness commonly not attributed to philosophical disputations?

Unlike the religious zealots who have God's commands on their minds, secular intellectuals have only the legacy of their predecessors in mind, otherwise it sounds like self-aggrandizing of the worst kind. The predicament of the Popperian legacy, in short, is that its call for public openness and individual freedom gets lost when the role models are eccentric and overbearing tyrants whose demeanour overshadows their sweet and passionate intent to help solve problems and make it a better world for us all.

Select bibliography

Ackermann, R. J. 1976. *The Philosophy of Karl Popper*. Amherst, MA: University of Massachusetts Press.

Adorno, T. *et al*. 1969. *The Positivist Dispute in German Sociology*. New York: Harper & Row.

Agassi, J. 1975. *Science in Flux*. Dordrecht: Reidel.

Agassi, J. 1981. *Science and Society: Studies in the Sociology of Science*. Dordrecht: Reidel.

Agassi, J. 1985. *Technology: Philosophical and Social Aspects*. Dordrecht: Reidel.

Agassi, J. 1991. "Deconstructing Post-Modernism: Gellner and Crocodile Dundee". In *Transition to Modernity: Essays on Power, Wealth and Belief, Gellner Festschrift*, J. A. Hall & I. C. Jarvie (eds), 213–30. Cambridge: Cambridge University Press.

Agassi, J. & Jarvie, I. (eds) 1987. *Rationality: The Critical View*. Dordrecht: Kluwer.

Bacon, F. [1620] 1985. *The New Organon*. New York: Macmillan.

Bloor, D. [1976] 1991. *Knowledge and Social Imagery*. Chicago, IL: University of Chicago Press.

Cornforth, M. 1968. *The Open Philosophy and the Open Society: A Reply to Dr. Karl Popper's Refutations of Marxism*. New York: International Publishers.

Corvi, R. 1997. *An Introduction to the Thought of Karl Popper*. Translated by Patrick Camiller. London: Routledge.

Dahl, R. A. 2001. *How Democratic Is the American Constitution?* New Haven, CT: Yale University Press.

Duhem, P. [1908] 1969. *To Save the Phenomena: An Essay on the Idea of Physical Theory from Plato to Galileo*. Translated by E. Dolan and C. Maschler. Chicago, IL: University of Chicago Press.

Edmonds, D. & Eidinow, J. 2001. *Wittgenstein's Poker: The Story of a Ten-Minute Argument Between Two Great Philosophers*. London: Faber.

Feyerabend, P. 1975. *Against Method: Outline of an Anarchistic Theory of Knowledge*. London: Verso.

Fuller, S. 2004. *Kuhn vs Popper: The Struggle for the Soul of Science*. New York: Columbia University Press.

Gellner, E. 1974. *Legitimation of Belief*. Cambridge: Cambridge University Press.

Gombrich, E. H. 1960. *Art and Illusion: A Study in the Psychology of Pictorial Representation*. Princeton, NJ: Princeton University Press.

Guattari, F. 1986. "The Postmodern Dead-End". *Flash Art* **128**: 40–41.

Hacohen, M. H. 2000. *Karl Popper: The Formative Years 1902–1945*. Cambridge: Cambridge University Press.

Haraway, D. 1991. *Simians, Cyborgs, and Women: The Reinvention of Nature*. London: Routledge.

Hausman, D. A. (ed.) 1984. *The Philosophy of Economics: An Anthology*. Cambridge: Cambridge University Press.

Hayek, F. A. [1944] 1976. *The Road to Serfdom: A Classical Warning against the Dangers to Freedom Inherent in Social Planning*. Chicago, IL: University of Chicago Press.

Hoesterey, I. (ed.) 1991. *Zeitgeist in Babel: The Postmodernist Controversy*. Bloomington, IN: Indiana University Press.

Hollis, M. & Nell, E. 1975. *Rational Economic Man: A Philosophical Critique of Neo-Classical Economics*. Cambridge: Cambridge University Press.

Jameson, F. 1991. *Postmodernism, or, The Cultural Logic of Late Capitalism*. Durham, NC: Duke University Press.

Jarvie, I. C. 1972. *Concepts and Society*. London: Routledge & Kegan Paul.

Jarvie, I. & Pralong, S. (eds) 1999. *Popper's Open Society After Fifty Years: The Continuing Relevance of Karl Popper*. London: Routledge.

Kuhn, T. [1962] 1970. *The Structure of Scientific Revolutions*. Chicago, IL: University of Chicago Press.

Lakatos, I. 1976. *Proofs and Refutations: The Logic of Mathematical Discovery*. Cambridge: Cambridge University Press.

Lakatos, I. & Musgrave, A. (eds) 1970. *Criticism and the Growth of Knowledge*. Cambridge: Cambridge University Press.

Laor, N. 1990. "Seduction in Tongues: Reconstructing the Field of Metaphor in the Treatment of Schizophrenia". In *Prescriptions: The Dissemination of Medical Authority*, G. Ormiston & R. Sassower (eds), 141–76. New York: Greenwood Press.

Levinson, R. B. 1957. *In Defense of Plato*. Cambridge: Cambridge University Press.

Lyotard, J-F. [1979] 1984. *The Postmodern Condition: A Report on Knowledge*. Translated by G. Bennington & B. Massumi. Minneapolis, MN: University of Minnesota Press.

Lyotard, J-F. [1988] 1990. *Heidegger and "the jews"*. Translated by A. Michel and M. Roberts. Minneapolis, MN: University of Minnesota Press.

Lyotard, J-F. [1983] 1988. *The Differend: Phrases in Dispute*. Translated by G. Van Den Abbeele. Minneapolis, MN: University of Minnesota Press.

Lyotard, J-F. & Thebaud, J-L. [1979] 1985. *Just Gaming*. Translated by W. Godzich. Minneapolis, MN: University of Minnesota Press.

Machlup, F. (ed.) 1977. *Essays on Hayek*. London: Routledge & Kegan Paul.

Magee, B. 1973. *Karl Popper*. New York: Viking.

Magee, B. 1985. *Philosophy and the Real World: An Introduction to Karl Popper*. LaSalle, IL: Open Court.

Menger, C. [1871] 1950. *Principles of Economics*. Translated and edited by James Dingwall and Bert H. Hoslitz. Glencoe, IL: Free Press.

Miller, D. (ed.) 1985. *Popper Selections*. Princeton, NJ: Princeton University Press.

Notturno, M. A. 2003. *On Popper*. Belmont, CA: Wadsworth.

O'Hear, A. 1980. *Karl Popper*. London: Routledge & Kegan Paul.

O'Hear, A. (ed.) 1995. *Karl Popper: Philosophy and Problems*. Cambridge: Cambridge University Press.

Orwell, G. [1946] 1956. *Animal Farm*. New York: Signet Classic.

Orwell, G. [1949] 1961. *1984*. New York: New American Library.

Plato 1975. *The Trial and Death of Socrates*. Translated by G. M. A. Grube. Indianapolis, IN: Hackett.

Polanyi, K. 1944. *The Great Transformation: The Political and Economic Origins of Our Time*. Boston, MA: Beacon Press.

Polanyi, M. 1958. *Personal Knowledge: Towards a Post-Critical Philosophy*. New York: Harper & Row.

Popper, K. 1957. *The Poverty of Historicism*. New York: Harper & Row.

Popper, K. [1935] 1959. *The Logic of Scientific Discovery*. New York: Harper & Row.

Popper, K. 1963. *Conjectures and Refutations: The Growth of Scientific Knowledge*. New York: Harper & Row.

Popper, K. [1943] 1966. *The Open Society and Its Enemies*. Volumes I and II. Princeton, NJ: Princeton University Press.

Popper, K. [1972] 1979. *Objective Knowledge: An Evolutionary Approach*. Oxford: Oxford University Press.

Popper, K. 1975. *Unended Quest: An Intellectual Autobiography*. La Salle, IL: Open Court.

Popper, K. 1999. *All Life is Problem Solving*. Translated by Patrick Camiller. London: Routledge.

Radnitzky, G. & Berhholz, P. (eds) 1987. *Economic Imperialism: The Economic Method Applied Outside the Field of Economics*. New York: Paragon House.

Radnitzky, G. & Bartley, W. W. III 1987. *Evolutionary Epistemology, Rationality, and the Sociology of Knowledge*. La Salle, IL: Open Court.

Russell, B. 1949. *Authority and the Individual*. Boston, MA: Beacon Press.

Sassower, R. 1985. *Philosophy of Economics: A Critique of Demarcation*. Lanham and New York: University Press of America.

Sassower, R. 1993. *Knowledge without Expertise: On the Status of Scientists*. Albany, NY: SUNY Press.

Sassower, R. 1995. *Cultural Collisions: Postmodern Technoscience*. New York: Routledge.

Sassower, R. 1997. *Technoscientific Angst: Ethics and Responsibility*. Minneapolis, MN: University of Minnesota Press.

Schilpp, A. (ed.) 1974. *The Philosophy of Karl Popper (2 volumes)*. LaSalle, IL: Open Court.

Schumpeter, J. A. 1977. *History of Economic Analysis*. New York: Oxford University Press.

Shearmur, J. 1996. *The Political Thought of Karl Popper*. London: Routledge.

Smith, A. [1776] 1937. *An Inquiry into the Nature and Causes of the Wealth of Nations*, edited by Edwin Cannan. New York: The Modern Library.

Soros, G. 2000. *Open Society: Reforming Global Capitalism*. New York: Public Affairs.

Strauss, L. & Cropsey, J. (eds) [1963] 1972. *History of Political Philosophy*. Chicago, IL: University of Chicago Press.

Toulmin, S. 1961. *Foresight and Understanding: An Enquiry into the Aims of Science*. London: Hutchinson.

Von Mises, L. [1922] 1981. *Socialism*. Translated by J. Kahane. Indianapolis, IN: Liberty Classics.

Von Mises, L. [1933] 1981. *Epistemological Problems of Economics*. Translated by George Reisman. New York: New York University Press.

Wartofsky, M. 1979. *Models: Representation and the Scientific Understanding*. Dordrecht: Reidel.

Weber, M. [1904–5] 1958. *The Protestant Ethic and the Spirit of Capitalism*. Translated by Talcott Parsons. New York: Scribner.

Williams, D. E. 1989. *Truth, Hope, and Power: The Thought of Karl Popper*. Toronto: University of Toronto Press.

Wolin, S. S. [1960] 2004. *Politics and Vision: Continuity and Innovation in Western Political Thought*. Princeton, NJ: Princeton University Press.

Zamiatin, E. (Y.) 1924. *WE*. Translated by Gregory Zilboorg. New York: Dutton.

Index